▶ **Soft Power and Freedom under the Coalition**

DOI: 10.1057/9781137505781.0001

Other Palgrave Pivot titles

David A. Savage and Benno Torgler: The Times They Are A Changin': The Effect of Institutional Change on Cooperative Behaviour at 26,000 ft over Sixty Years

Mike Finn (editor): The Gove Legacy: Education in Britain after the Coalition

Clive D. Field: Britain's Last Religious Revival? Quantifying Belonging, Behaving, and Believing in the Long 1950s

Richard Rose and Caryn Peiffer: Paying Bribes for Public Services: A Global Guide to Grass-Roots Corruption

Altug Yalcintas: Creativity and Humour in Occupy Movements: Intellectual Disobedience in Turkey and Beyond

Joanna Black, Juan Carlos Castro, and Ching-Chiu Lin: Youth Practices in Digital Arts and New Media: Learning in Formal and Informal Settings

Wouter Peeters, Andries De Smet, Lisa Diependaele and Sigrid Sterckx: Climate Change and Individual Responsibility: Agency, Moral Disengagement and the Motivational Gap

Mark Stelzner: Economic Inequality and Policy Control in the United States

Michelle Bayefsky and Bruce Jennings: Regulating Preimplantation Genetic Diagnosis in the United States

Eileen Piggot-Irvine: Goal Pursuit in Education Using Focused Action Research

Serenella Massidda: Audiovisual Translation in the Digital Age: The Italian Fansubbing Phenomenon

John Board, Alfonso Dufour, Yusuf Hartavi, Charles Sutcliffe and Stephen Wells: Risk and Trading on London's Alternative Investment Market: The Stock Market for Smaller and Growing Companies

Franklin G. Mixon, Jr: Public Choice Economics and the Salem Witchcraft Hysteria

Elisa Menicucci: Fair Value Accounting: Key Issues Arising from the Financial Crisis

Nicoletta Pireddu: The Works of Claudio Magris: Temporary Homes, Mobile Identities, European Borders

Larry Patriquin: Economic Equality and Direct Democracy in Ancient Athens

Antoine Pécoud: Depoliticising Migration: Global Governance and International Migration Narratives

Gerri Kimber: Katherine Mansfield and the Art of the Short Story: A Literary Modernist

C. Paul Hallwood and Thomas J. Miceli: Maritime Piracy and its Control: An Economic Analysis

Letizia Guglielmo and Lynée Lewis Gaillet (editors): Contingent Faculty Publishing in Community: Case Studies for Successful Collaborations

palgrave▸pivot

Soft Power and Freedom under the Coalition: State-Corporate Power and the Threat to Democracy

Emma Bell
Université de Savoie, France

palgrave
macmillan

DOI: 10.1057/9781137505781.0001

First published 2015 by
PALGRAVE MACMILLAN

Palgrave Macmillan in the UK is an imprint of Macmillan Publishers Limited, registered in England, company number 785998, of Houndmills, Basingstoke, Hampshire RG21 6XS.

Palgrave Macmillan in the US is a division of St Martin's Press LLC, 175 Fifth Avenue, New York, NY 10010.

Palgrave Macmillan is the global academic imprint of the above companies and has companies and representatives throughout the world.

Palgrave® and Macmillan® are registered trademarks in the United States, the United Kingdom, Europe and other countries.

ISBN: 978–1–137–50579–8 EPUB
ISBN: 978–1–137–50578–1 PDF
ISBN: 978–1–137–50577–4 Hardback

A catalogue record for this book is available from the British Library.

A catalog record for this book is available from the Library of Congress.

www.palgrave.com/pivot

DOI: 10.1057/9781137505781

Contents

DOI: 10.1057/9781137505781.0001

Acknowledgements

Thanks to all those whose political commitment and curiosity helped to inspire the writing of this book, especially friends from the European Group for the Study of Deviance and Social Control. Sara Crowley Vigneau and Jemima Warren at Palgrave Macmillan were particularly professional and helpful. Huge thanks to Keith Dixon, Gilles Christoph and Neil Davie for helping to edit the final manuscript and for their constant support and encouragement. Finally, of course, I'd like to thank my friends and family, especially John, for obvious reasons.

List of Relevant UK Legislation

Academies Act 2010
Anti-social Behaviour Crime and Policing Act 2014
Criminal Justice Act 2003
Criminal Justice and Public Order Act 1994
Data Retention and Regulatory Powers Act 2014
Enterprise and Regulatory Reform Act 2013
European Union Act 2011
Financial Services Act 2012
Financial Services (Banking Reform) Act 2013
Freedom of Information Act 2000
Growth and Infrastructure Act 2013
Health and Social Care Act 2012
Human Rights Act 1998
Identity Cards Act 2006
Identity Documents Act 2010
Justice and Security Act 2013
Legal Aid, Sentencing and Punishment of Offenders
    Act 2012
Local Government Act 1988
Localism Act 2011
Marriage (Same Sex Couples Act) 2013
Organised Crime and Police Act 2005
Police and Criminal Evidence Act 1984
Protection of Freedoms Act 2012
Regulation of Investigatory Powers Act 2000
Social Value Act 2012
Terrorism Act 2000
Terrorism Act 2006

DOI: 10.1057/9781137505781.0003

Terrorist Prevention and Investigation Measures (TPIMs) Act 2013
Transparency of Lobbying, Non-party Campaigning and Trade Union
   Administration Act 2014
Welfare Reform Act 2012

DOI: 10.1057/9781137505781.0003

palgrave▶pivot

Introduction:
A Liberal Manifesto

Bell, Emma. *Soft Power and Freedom under the Coalition: State-Corporate Power and the Threat to Democracy.* Basingstoke: Palgrave Macmillan, 2015. DOI: 10.1057/9781137505781.0004.

▶

During the 13 years that New Labour was in power, critics on both the left and the right of the political spectrum asserted that there had been a steady erosion of basic freedoms in Britain, coupled with a rise in the power and reach of the state. Despite implementing wide-ranging constitutional reform leading to the decentralisation of power from Westminster to the regions, successive governments since 1997 were accused of having concentrated political power at the centre. Tony Blair was thought to have personalised power to such an extent that there was much debate about whether or not the functions of the British Prime Minister were being 'presidentialised' (Foley, 2002; Heffernan, 2005). It was feared that he was sidelining Cabinet, the civil service and collective ministerial decision-making, often favouring the advice of unelected policy advisers over that of elected ministers. Writing at the end of the Blair government's first term of office, Margaret Thatcher complained that his government was 'overweening', 'sustained by cronies, ciphers and a personality cult' and revived Lord Hailsham's 1976 warning (Hailsham, 1976) that Britain was in danger of slipping into an 'elective dictatorship' (Thatcher, 2001). Furthermore, despite having passed the *Human Rights Act 1998*, allowing British citizens to uphold their rights in British courts without having to go before the European Court in Strasbourg, New Labour was thought by some to have seriously undermined civil liberties. In particular, it strengthened the powers of the State vis-à-vis the ordinary citizen, limiting the right to protest, developing a national identity register and ID card scheme, expanding stop-and-search powers, blurring the boundaries between the civil and criminal law and eroding basic legal protections, notably allowing the detention without trial of foreign terrorist suspects. The result was that the power of ordinary citizens appeared to have been eroded in favour of the strengthened power of the State. On announcing his bid for leadership of the Labour Party in May 2010, Ed Miliband conceded that the party had been too 'casual' 'about the relation between the state and the individual' (Miliband, 2010).

But it was the newly formed Conservative–Liberal Democrat coalition government that was to attempt to take up the mantle of civil liberties, to usher in 'a new politics', bringing about 'an historic and seismic shift in our political landscape', a key element of which would be a commitment to civil liberties and 'curbing the power of the state' (Cameron, 2010a). Alongside fairness and responsibility, freedom was to be a central plank of the new programme for government. Consequently, the new Coalition committed itself to 'shift[ing] power from Westminster to people'. This would entail promoting 'decentralisation and democratic engagement' and an 'end [to] the era of top-down government by giving new powers to local councils, communities, neighbourhoods and individuals' (HM Government, 2010a: 11). Reducing the power of the State in favour of individuals was presented as the key to solving Britain's problems. According to the coalition's narrative, a bloated state had not just eroded civil liberties and excluded ordinary citizens from politics but was responsible for the apparently desperate economic situation Britain was facing in 2010 (which the new government claimed had been caused by overspending) and for social problems such as welfare dependency and crime (which the government claimed had undermined personal and social responsibility). For Cameron, 'the size, scope and role of government in Britain ha[d] reached a point where it [was] now inhibiting, not advancing the progressive aims of reducing poverty, fighting inequality, and increasing general wellbeing' (2009).

Reducing the role of the State was not only a 'liberal' manifesto in the sense that it aimed to restore freedom to individuals but it was also a progressive one. It was, importantly for the Conservatives, a way for the party to 'detoxify' its image as the 'nasty party' while simultaneously tapping in to traditional conservative fears about the over-powerful state. Yet, this was not just about electoral opportunism (Bale, 2010). There was a serious attempt to develop a new philosophical direction for the party, symbolised in particular by the work of the Centre for Social Justice, established by former party leader Iain Duncan Smith in 2004 to develop a conservative response to social problems, and by the work of Conservative intellectuals and MPs such as Jesse Norman and David Willetts who helped elaborate key ideas such as 'civic' and 'compassionate conservatism ' and the 'Big Society' (Ganesh & Norman, 2006; Norman, 2010; Willetts, 1994). Underpinning all this work was a strong belief that the role of the State should be reduced in order to set people free. But the aim was not to promote the rampant individualism that had seemed to mark the Thatcher years, damaging the conservatives' reputation and breaking down the bonds that tie society together. Freedom was to be promoted by encouraging responsibility, not just for oneself, but also towards others. This idea was key to the 'Big Society' that Cameron hoped would be promoted via a reduction in state power.

As for the Liberal Democrats, prior to assuming power in 2010 they had carried out their own reassessment of the values that should guide

DOI: 10.1057/9781137505781.0004

their party. While emphasising their traditional commitment to civil liberties and constitutional reform, they sought to reassert their commitment to economic liberalism. In *The Orange Book* (Marshall & Laws, 2004), senior Liberal Democrats, including the deputy prime minister, sought to reduce the role of the State in order to encourage public service reform which would give a greater role to the private sector while also encouraging individual responsibility and initiative.

Both parties to the Coalition have placed more emphasis on negative liberty, freedom *from* state interference (Berlin in Hardy, 2002, p. 174). The Conservative Party in particular has traditionally subscribed to this notion of freedom, as it has been unwilling to place unnecessary restrictions on individuals within the limits of the rule of law (Dorey, 2011, p. 20). The New Liberals of H. H. Asquith have often been associated more with what Berlin described as 'positive liberty', namely, the freedom *to* be one's 'own master' (Berlin in Hardy, 2002, p. 178). For New Liberals such as Leonard Hobhouse, 'nominal freedom' from restraint was insufficient to secure 'effective liberty' (Hobhouse, 1911). State intervention was therefore justified to guarantee a number of 'positive' freedoms, notably freedom from poverty. Even Conservatives have at times endorsed the idea of positive freedom. Macmillan, for example, suggested that they could simultaneously defend economic freedom while preserving the positive freedoms initially developed by the New Liberals in the form of the welfare state (Green, 2002, p. 172). Today, both Liberals and Conservatives accept some forms of positive liberty, notably the freedom of all to marry, regardless of sexual orientation. State intervention is even accepted to guarantee effective freedom from discrimination. Yet, most discussion of freedom within both parties focuses on reducing the role of the State in favour of both the freedom of the market and of individuals from government interference. This is regardless of the fact that in practice the State continues to intervene in the market to guarantee effective positive freedoms to big business.

Rolling back the State is often regarded as a means of automatically restoring freedom to individuals. It is a zero-sum game: the more power accrues to the State, the less power accrues to individuals and vice versa. For the coalition government, power and freedom were regarded as synonymous. Yet, freedom is not absolute: the State continues to define the parameters of how it is used, ensuring that it is used responsibly. As Cameron explained, 'the stifling clutch of state control [would] be replaced by the transformative power of social responsibility' (2010b).

The Big State was to be replaced by the Big Society. It was not just individuals who were to benefit from less state intervention but also communities and local authorities who were expected to work together, often with the private sector, to bring about social change.

This short book seeks to assess to what extent this 'liberal' manifesto was realised over the course of the Coalition's five-year mandate. It focuses on five main policy areas. It begins by looking at whether trends towards the centralisation of power, dating back even before the New Labour era, were halted, focusing on the peculiar circumstances of coalition government, linking current trends to theories of governance, and evaluating the impact of the localism agenda on the exercise of the power of the central state (Chapter 1). It then looks at whether or not ordinary citizens, notably the poor, have really been empowered via social policy measures which sought to encourage individual responsibility and 'active citizenship' (Chapter 2). The discussion moves on to an analysis of the government's policies on civil liberties and crime, looking at whether the 'right' balance was indeed found between liberty and security (Chapter 3). Economic policy is then analysed, focusing on policies of austerity and privatisation and the increased role accorded to the private sector as the means of securing economic recovery (Chapter 4). Finally, the contours of 'liberal' foreign policy are traced, notably looking at how the British state has continued to further its interests abroad in partnership with the private sector via the exercise of soft, as opposed to hard, power (Chapter 5).

The term 'soft power' is generally only used to refer to states' exercise of power abroad (Nye, 2004), as a way of extending cultural and economic influence without the use of military intervention. However, this book seeks to broaden the application of the term to include the exercise of state power at home through more subtle means than those deployed by classically authoritarian governments. 'Soft power' here is understood as more diffuse, exercised via the intermediary of a number of different State and non-State actors. It is less overtly coercive, and tends to be dressed in the language of individual empowerment. Yet, it is demonstrated that shifting responsibility onto individuals and communities does not necessarily result in more freedom and empowerment. Indeed, the central thesis of the book is that liberal discourse has been used to justify continued authoritarianism: the liberal discourse of localism has masked the continued directive power of the central state and the privileging of corporate over local power; liberal 'compassionate' conservative

DOI: 10.1057/9781137505781.0004

social policies have masked the degree of state and corporate coercion of vulnerable populations; illiberal anti-terror and pre-crime measures have been disguised in the liberal discourse of security whereby the state's primary role is seen as protecting the individual from external threats (Neocleous, 2007); the politics of austerity which responsibilise individual citizens has been justified by the liberal discourse of the free market; and new imperialistic measures extending both state and corporate power have been dressed in the liberal language of international aid and development. This is the liberal politics of paradox: the continued exercise of state authoritarianism under the guise of liberalism. Foucault long ago highlighted this paradox, pointing to the illiberal consequences of liberal rule, but his focus was primarily on the State (Foucault in Burchell et al., 1991). While this book does not deny the role of the State, it seeks to extend analysis to looking at the unprecedented power of the private sector as a partner in governance and the impact that this has had on individual freedom. It regards the rise of corporate power as being the essential determining feature of neoliberalism as opposed to previous forms of liberalism. This is not to suggest that there has been some form of trade-off between state and corporate power but rather that each form of power helps to reinforce the other. The book ends by looking at the nefarious consequences this may have on democracy before attempting to suggest some exit strategies which would allow us to move beyond the politics of liberal authoritarianism.

DOI: 10.1057/9781137505781.0004

1
Decentring the State

Abstract: *The chapter aims to determine whether or not power has really been devolved from the central state by analysing the peculiarities of coalition politics and the coalition's localism agenda. It is suggested that localism has largely been a failure in terms of genuinely transferring power from central government to local people. But the strategy has been effective in terms of allowing the government to divest itself of responsibility for policy failure via the responsibilisation of local institutions while opening up new markets for the private sector. The localism agenda may more accurately be considered as a strategy of governmentality than one of simple governance owing to the way in which it seeks to use non-governmental actors to pursue its own agenda.*

Keywords: governance; governmentality; localism

Bell, Emma. *Soft Power and Freedom under the Coalition: State-Corporate Power and the Threat to Democracy.* Basingstoke: Palgrave Macmillan, 2015.
DOI: 10.1057/9781137505781.0005.

At the heart of the new coalition government's plan to shift power from the State to the people was decentralisation. It aimed to reform government at the centre and to devolve decision-making from central government to local communities. This chapter seeks to determine whether or not the coalition succeeded in 'decentring the State' and consequently in empowering local communities. It looks at how such an agenda should have been facilitated by the very fact of coalition politics which necessarily implied a move away from the personalisation and over-centralisation of power, so closely associated with the Blair and Thatcher eras. It then discusses the impact of trends away from government by the centre to governance by a range of different institutions, asking whether this has aided the coalition's decentralisation agenda. Next, the details of the government's localism agenda are analysed to determine if they have genuinely led to a shift in power dynamics in Britain in favour of local government and communities.

Power-sharing and democratic government

A number of commentators were hopeful that the arrival of coalition government would herald a very different form of politics from the *dirigisme* that had characterised the New Labour years. Some hoped that the need for consensual, democratic decision-making between the two parties to government would lead to a revival of Cabinet government whereby decisions would be taken collectively by senior ministers and Cabinet Office would serve the Cabinet as a whole, not merely the prime minister, as was often said to have been the case under Blair (Brockwell, 2010; Blick & Jones, 2010, p. 175). It was hoped that rather than decisions being taken unilaterally or bilaterally, often with unelected special advisers instead of with democratically elected ministers (Anderson & Mann, 1997, p. 51; Byrne & Weir, 2004, p. 458), they would be taken by the Cabinet as a whole. Others have suggested that Cameron's personal prime ministerial power was considerably weakened by the fact of coalition, asserting that 'unlike past predominant prime ministers such as Thatcher and Blair, [he was] often unable to fully assert himself on either his party or government' (Bennister & Heffernan, 2014: 15). Indeed, his prerogative powers of ministerial appointment were severely restricted by the fact that he was obliged to appoint a fair number of Liberal Democrats to Cabinet and had to leave the reshuffling of those ministers

DOI: 10.1057/9781137505781.0005

to his Deputy, Nick Clegg (ibid., p. 3). Clearly, the weakening of power at the very centre of British politics does not necessarily restore power to the people – it may be that power is merely diffused among a range of other political and non-political actors. However, it may strengthen accountability mechanisms, ensuring that democratically elected members of government are primarily responsible for political decision-making, thus restoring the health of democracy. Before power can be shared with members of civil society, it must first be shared at the top.

Yet, in practice, the weakening of prime ministerial power in Britain did not lead to a corresponding strengthening of Cabinet power. While decision-making had to be shared between two parties, it was not shared across government as a whole but remained very much concentrated at the centre, with the majority of decisions being taken by the so-called 'Quad' or 'inner Cabinet' (Hazell, 2012), comprised of the prime minister, the deputy prime minister, the chancellor and the chief secretary to the Treasury (David Cameron, Nick Clegg, George Osborne and Danny Alexander). This has been described as a 'semi-formal institution' where many of the most important coalition policy issues, particularly those with spending implications, were resolved before they were discussed in the more formal institutions of the Cabinet and the Coalition Committee (ibid., 2012). This does not, however, mean that Cabinet was sidelined – according to Hazell, it became an important final stage in signing off policy agreements, even if these were mostly worked out beforehand via informal mechanisms. Yet, nor does it mean that power at the centre was weakened. Indeed, it is alleged that 'the Quad ... limited other ministers' freedom to manoeuvre [since] decisions taken by the Quad [were] handed down to other ministers to implement' (Montgomerie, 2012). Although both parties to the coalition were equally represented in this closed circle, representing a true instance of coalition power-sharing, with Liberal Democrat views being given much more credence than their numerical presence in government merited, it is reminiscent of the 'Big Four' comprised of the most influential personalities in the early years of the Blair government (the then Prime Minister Tony Blair, Chancellor Gordon Brown, the Deputy Prime Minister John Prescott and the Foreign Secretary Robin Cook). Indeed, decision-making through the Quad was criticised as a coalition version of Blair's 'sofa government' whereby decisions were taken informally by select ministers and advisers working outside the Cabinet system (House of Lords Select Committee on the Constitution, 2014, p. 27). In further continuity with

DOI: 10.1057/9781137505781.0005

the Blair years, the 'Quad' tended to work in close coordination with a range of unelected 'experts', including special advisers, strategists and media communications experts who make up part of Cameron's 'inner circle'. These included a number of Old Etonians and personal friends of the prime minister, notably Oliver Letwin, minister for government policy; Jo Johnson, head of his policy unit; Ed Llewellyn, chief of staff; and Rupert Harrison, George Osborne's chief economic adviser (Parker & Warrell, 2014). According to Anthony Seldon, they 'effectively [ran] Number Ten' (Seldon, 2011), suggesting that the political cronyism of the Blair years has been alive and well in the coalition government.

The extent to which power was truly shared with the Liberal Democrats is also questionable, despite the existence of the informal 'Quad' and the more formal coalition committee. The latter, jointly chaired by Cameron and Clegg was set up to solve coalition disputes, but it hardly ever met, informal mechanisms being much more important (Constitution Unit, 2011: 4). There is a general consensus that the Conservatives have remained the dominant partners in the coalition, imposing a number of so-called 'red line issues', policies which are not up for negotiation. These include foreign policy (Honeyman, 2012), Europe (Lynch, 2012, p. 77), immigration (Bale & Hampshire, 2012, p. 102) and economic policy (Gamble, 2012a, p. 64). With regard to the latter, Hay argued, 'for "the Conservative–Liberal Democrat Coalition" one can practically substitute the will of the Conservative leadership. For, it is difficult to see how the process of coalition formation...tempered, in any significant respect, any aspect of Conservative economic policy' (Hay, 2010, p. 394). As is demonstrated in Chapter 4, they actively supported policy in this respect, yet failed to lead it. The fact of being in coalition enabled the Conservatives to legitimate their economic policies of austerity, forcing their political allies to share the blame for the pain inflicted by the cuts while reaping the electoral rewards resulting from an apparent improvement in the economic fortunes of the country (Hayton, 2013, p. 16). Overall, the Liberal Democrats failed to secure key pledges on electoral and Lords reform, and while the Party did manage to spearhead specific policies such as an increase in the tax threshold above which people begin paying income tax, these seem insignificant compared to wide-ranging reform programmes led by the Conservatives (Dommett, 2013, pp. 224–5). So, rather than implementing a new form of bi-partisan politics with greater democratic legitimacy than single-party governments (the coalition parties together commanded 59 per cent of the popular

DOI: 10.1057/9781137505781.0005

vote at the 2010 election), it would appear that coalition politics actually helped the Conservatives to remain dominant, thus allowing Cameron to strengthen his power at the centre.

The power of government more generally was also strengthened by reforms to the civil service which, far from 'improving the civil service' as a way of fixing the 'broken' political system (HM Government, 2010a, pp. 26–7), actually threaten to undermine its independence. As of 2013, government ministers were given the discretionary power to appoint their own civil servants, special advisers and external appointees to new 'Extended Ministerial Offices' (Civil Service, 2013, p. 31). Civil servants appointed to these offices fulfil very similar roles to those exercised by existing permanent secretaries, helping to formulate policy and handling communications; yet, unlike the latter, they are accountable only to the ministers who appoint them rather than to Parliament as a whole. The government aim was to strengthen accountability mechanisms by making the lines of political accountability more clear-cut but there are fears that this reform will exacerbate the politicisation of Whitehall whereby ministers and civil servants alike are 'more driven by the news agenda' than hitherto (Jenkin, 2014, p. 88). Civil servants will find it hard to disagree with the ministers on whom they depend. As one former civil servant argues:

> [Extended Ministerial Offices], and those who work within them, would be bound to become extensions of the minister's personality and beliefs. The real risk is that counter-arguments, difficult facts and embarrassing truths would be much less likely to reach the table, as would officials willing to tell it as it is. (Lewis, 2014, p. 85)

Under such circumstances, it would be extremely difficult for these new civil servants to provide politically impartial advice in the public interest when that is thought to conflict with the political priorities of ministers. Indeed, they may soon lack the expertise that would enable them to do so now that all new permanent secretaries are appointed on fixed-term contracts. As their name suggests, permanent secretaries were previously appointed for indeterminate periods, allowing them to accumulate expertise. In theory, this system was also meant to ensure their political impartiality since they would usually remain in office for much longer than the usual term of a single government. Indeed, the Civil Service Code of Conduct, drawn up in 2010, specifically highlights the need for political impartiality, stating that the role of all civil servants is to 'serve the Government, whatever its political persuasion to the best of [their] ability in a way which maintains political impartiality and is in line with the requirements of this Code, no matter what [their] own political beliefs are' (Civil Service, 2010). Yet, an internal civil service document outlining the main qualities required to be a permanent secretary provoked controversy by suggesting that such officials should place the long-term aims of their department over that of their ministers or the government as a whole (Civil Service, 2014).

These civil service reforms reflect the growing complexity of government – indeed, the government itself justified the need for reform specifically on the grounds that 'the pace and complexity of government [is] ever increasing' (Civil Service, 2013, p. 31). This may suggest that decentralisation, whether actively implemented or not, is inevitable as power is devolved to an increasingly wide range of institutions. It has certainly become very difficult to retain power at the centre on account of the growth in the size of government over the last century to include not just ministers and a greatly extended civil service but also, more recently, a vast number of 'quangoes', quasi non-governmental organisations, and even private contractors providing public services on behalf of government (Weir & Beetham, 1999, pp. 132–3). It may even be suggested that the diffusion of power from the centre that these changes necessarily entail may lead to the greater democratic participation of the people, allowing them to become truly active citizens, thus freeing them from the power of the Central State.

Such a theory may seem to be supported by the shift from *government* to *governance*, a trend that has been much commented upon since at least the 1990s. The term 'governance' has a multitude of meanings. Rhodes, one of the most prolific writers on the subject, has identified at least six possible meanings of the term: as the minimal state involving at least the rhetorical reduction in the powers of the State; as corporate governance, with reference to new, accountable management structures; as new public management, involving the transfer of market principles to the public sector; as 'good governance', focusing on the accountability and the efficiency of state institutions; as a socio-cybernetic system, whereby a multiplicity of actors formulate and implement policy together; and as self-organising networks, understood as autonomous networks of organisations in the public, private and voluntary sectors working relatively independently to deliver policy goals (Rhodes, 1996). What all these definitions have in common is that they, to at least some extent, entail

DOI: 10.1057/9781137505781.0005

diluting the power of the State or, as Rhodes would have it, 'hollowing out the state' (Rhodes, 1994). Osborne and Gaebler also captured this notion when they argued that government's role should move from that of 'rowing' to 'steering', meaning that government should dismantle the bureaucratic, centralised State and retreat from service delivery, instead contracting out delivery to non-state actors and contenting itself with controlling the general direction of policy implementation (1993). The discourse of governance may thus be regarded as a liberal discourse in the sense that it seeks to free individuals and other organisations from the absolute control of a central, sovereign State. For Bevir, it is a specifically neoliberal discourse, one that favours a more entrepreneurial pattern of rule and provides a solid justification for minimal state interference in the market and beyond (Bevir, 2010: 30). Governance can therefore be regarded as a reaction against the post-war 'overloaded' (King, 1975) 'rowing' State and the political consensus that accompanied it, characterised as it was by 'club government' (Marquand, 1988) in which policy formulation was highly centralised within a tight-knit community of highly educated administrative experts. On this understanding, it may seem that it is through governance that 'decentralisation and democratic engagement' can best be promoted. Yet, as is demonstrated below, this has not been the case in practice.

The governance of freedom

Governance entails transferring power to a multiplicity of actors, involving the public, private and voluntary sectors in the practice of government. Governance thus sits well with influential pluralist accounts of the State which highlight the centrality of groups to the political process, regarding the State as just one political actor among others (Smith, 2006). In these accounts, power is considered to be truly diffuse and shared among all actors involved in the political process. Governance is thus regarded as a very positive political development, as it fits perfectly with liberal notions of how a truly democratic State should behave. Yet, as Smith points out, following Marsh (2002), plurality does not necessarily mean pluralism since 'the existence of many groups and policy domains does not mean that power is dispersed and that access is open' (Smith, 2006, p. 30). The same goes for governance: we should be very wary of engaging in zero-sum games, assuming that an increase in the role of

DOI: 10.1057/9781137505781.0005

the private sector, for example, automatically equates with a diminishing role for the State (Lister & Marsh, 2006, p. 255). Rather than regarding the trend towards involving a greater multiplicity of actors in governance as diminishing the power of the State, as the neoliberal reformers of the 1980s and 1990s had hoped, it would be more appropriate to regard this trend as having led to a 'congested state' in which the State remains largely in control of an increasingly complex structure of partnerships and networks (Skelcher, 2000). Indeed, the proliferation of policy networks, particularly under the Blair government, is often heavily criticised by the neoliberal reformers who hoped that reforms in governance would lead to the creation of pure markets in public services, free of State interference (Bevir, 2010, p. 33). Yet, if the power of the State has not diminished, the power of the private sector has undoubtedly been on the rise to the detriment of civil society organisations, a point that will be examined in detail in Chapter 4. Accounts of governance need to recognise that some groups are more powerful than others.

The State remains the most powerful actor of all. Indeed, for a number of commentators, claims that the State has been weakened by governance are dubious. Peters and Pierre, for example, have claimed that 'rumours of the death of the State are exaggerated' (2006, p. 221). For Peters, the notion of governance without government is a myth: it is the State that grants power to other actors in governance and can just as easily revoke it (Peters, 1997: 57). Indeed, 'the authority the State gives to non-state actors is only ever on loan' (Bell & Hindmoor, 2009, p. 9). Furthermore, regardless of widespread popular criticism of the State, citizens will always expect government to step in when things go wrong (ibid., pp. 15, 31). For example, governments will always be called upon to address problems in the market (Peters, 1997, p. 54), never more so than in the wake of the most recent financial crisis (see Chapter 4). For Bell and Hindmoor, states remain responsible for 'metagovernance', even when they govern through markets, associations and civil society. They describe this as the 'government of governance' (2009, p. 11). Metagovernance entails the State steering (setting goals for other political actors to meet); measuring effectiveness (determining the evaluative criteria that will determine the success or failure of a particular policy/ service); providing resources (be these financial, administrative or coercive); ensuring that democratic principles are respected (guaranteeing legitimacy and the participation of civil society); providing accountability mechanisms (since it is government that is ultimately held to

DOI: 10.1057/9781137505781.0005

account when things go wrong); and promoting legitimacy (generating confidence and trust in new governance structures) (ibid., pp. 46–55). Only government has the capacity to assume such a function of oversight and general management, largely on account of its monopoly of the legitimate use of violence, meaning that the State alone has the necessary powers of coercion to ensure that governance actors comply with certain rules and regulations (ibid., pp. 55–6).

So, rather than state power being in retreat, it has in reality been transformed and even enhanced, as the subsequent discussion seeks to demonstrate, using concrete examples. This idea is captured in Moran's notion of the 'regulatory state' (Moran, 2007), suggesting that while the State may have contracted out governance to other institutions, suggesting a reduced role for the state, it actually retains an important metagovernance role of regulation, ensuring that those institutions comply with basic rules and standards. An example may be given of private companies who are constantly subject to regulatory control to ensure that they meet certain goals and targets set by the State. But regulation also extends into civil society. Here, regulation can be both liberating and coercive. King provides the example of new regulations ensuring compliance with Human Rights legislation which operate alongside coercive regulations which seek to change the behaviour of the governed, such as antisocial behaviour legislation which uses the threat of penal sanctions to force conformity with certain norms (King, 2007, p. 66). Yet, more regulation is enforced via 'soft words' rather than 'big sticks' (ibid.). State power is to be exercised through 'soft power', through persuasion rather than outright repression. This entails replacing destructive repressive power with productive disciplinary power, in the Foucauldian sense of the term, whereby individuals are to be encouraged to change their behaviour in such a way that they can be more effectively governed (Bell & Hindmoor, 2009, p. 98). As the government promised in 2010, it would move beyond 'rules and regulations' as means of changing people's behaviour, adopting 'smarter' strategies of government that [would] instead find 'intelligent ways to encourage, support and enable people to make better choices for themselves' (HM Government, 2010a, pp. 7–8). It is the State that possesses the necessary resources, notably the powers of coercion, necessary to effect such changes over the individual (Bell & Hindmoor, 2009, p. 99). But other actors in governance, notably actors in civil society, may also participate and may be perceived as more legitimate given their perceived distance from State power.

DOI: 10.1057/9781137505781.0005

According to this view, the principal aim of liberal government is to create free, responsible individuals. If there is coercion and regulation, it is therefore exercised only in the name of freedom (Rose, 1996, p. 41) – governing freedom becomes the chief object of governance (see Chapter 2). The State does this with many other actors – the neoliberal State tends to prioritise the private sector whereas the liberal State tended to favour working in partnership with a range of social science experts – but it remains central for the reasons outlined earlier. It determines exactly how its partners in governance encourage people to harness their own freedom. Perhaps the term 'governmentality' is more appropriate than that of 'governance' to describe contemporary practices of government. It encapsulates this notion of the centrality of the State in manipulating the technologies of government that spread throughout society. As Foucault understood it, governmentality refers to 'the ensemble formed by the institutions, procedures, analyses and reflections, the calculations and tactics that allow the exercise of this very specific albeit complex form of power'; 'the formation of a whole series of specific governmental apparatuses' (Foucault, 1978, pp. 102–3). It is the development of these new, diffuse ways of exercising power that has permitted the State to adapt to the increasingly complex task of government. Today, it is the discourse of localism and decentralisation that legitimises the exercise of state power.

Governing through the 'Big Society'

In many ways, the coalition's programme of localism may be regarded as a perfect example of governmentality (Davoudi & Madanipour, 2013) in the sense that it ostensibly aims to create free, responsible citizens, capable of improving their local communities without the need for excessive state intervention, while in reality the coercive power of the central state is pervasive. The project of localism was marketed under the banner of the 'Big Society'. This broad, perhaps deliberately ambiguous, term enabled the Conservative Party to distinguish its agenda from that of the Thatcher years by suggesting that it would henceforth be more interested in society, in its problems and its public services. While Cameron echoed Thatcher in claiming that society is not the same thing as the State (Cameron, 2005), he sought to go beyond Thatcherism by putting forward an agenda that would not just focus on reducing the

DOI: 10.1057/9781137505781.0005

power of the State but also on increasing the power of society. The Big Society project was thus to be primarily about decentralisation, a means of 'pushing power and control away from the centre and into communities and neighbourhoods' (Maude, 2011). Thatcher of course also hoped to give individuals more power through her policy of 'rolling back the state', giving them more choice over public service provision and allowing them to become shareholders and home-owners. Blair sought to empower individuals via 'communitarian' policies (Etzioni, 1995) such as 'active citizenship' which would revive the 'civic virtues' of responsibility. Cameron's Conservatives, supported by the Liberal Democrats, aimed to go further by encouraging individuals *and* local communities to get involved in improving society themselves. There were two main prongs to this agenda – the reform of public services and the *Localism Act 2011*. Both policies were intended to empower individuals by promoting localism. Yet, 'setting the people free' would paradoxically entail significant direction from the Central State. As Cameron himself put it, 'the big society is not just going to spring into life on its own: we need strong and concerted government action to make it happen. We need to use the state to remake society' (2009). True to his word, the State took on a central coordinating role, revealing an authoritarian flipside to the apparently liberal Big Society agenda.

Let us first take the example of public services. The most significant reforms under the Big Society agenda were made in education and in health. In education, parents were to be given more choice and professionals more chance 'to innovate' (Cameron, 2011a). The means of doing so were provided by the *Academies Act 2010* which allowed all state schools in England to apply for 'academy status', essentially allowing them to become free of local authority and central government control, by giving them the power to choose how to manage their own finances, to determine the curriculum (provided it is 'broad and balanced') and to determine teachers' pay and conditions. By November 2014, there were 4,296 academies either open or in development (Department for Education, 2014), compared to just 203 in May 2010 (HM Government, 2010). Furthermore, the 2010 Act allowed academies to be supplemented by 'free schools', schools that can have the same status as academies but which are set up on the initiative of teachers, parents, charities, religious or voluntary groups. They are directly funded by the government but are run by charitable trusts which may invite private investment or outsource the running of schools to for-profit providers, as was the case

DOI: 10.1057/9781137505781.0005

for Breckland Middle School. Twenty-four free schools were opened in September 2011 – by January 2014, the number had increased to more than 3,000 (Gove, 2014).

In practice, these new schools are not as 'free' as their name suggests. Although exempt from some central government rules and regulations, they are not exempt from regulatory powers, such as mandatory inspections by the official education regulator, Ofsted. Such controls are obviously desirable to ensure that pupils' interests are being protected, yet a further form of regulation does not appear to put either pupils' or teachers' interests first. This is the requirement for every free school to be fully subscribed. If they fail to attract the requisite number of pupils, they will have their funding cut. This 'implies that their autonomy is constrained by the need to attract customers in the education quasi-market' (Leeder & Mabbett, 2012, p. 135). Furthermore, in common with academies and state schools, they are to be subjected to market-inspired pressures to meet key performance indicators (ibid., p. 135). As Griffiths points out, the *Academies Act* was essentially about the State subjecting schools to market pressures, thus preventing them from being truly 'free' (2011, p. 79).

The same can be said for universities which, following the Commons vote in November 2010 to implement the recommendations of the Browne Review, have been permitted to increase tuition fees (originally introduced under the first Blair government) to up to £9,000 per year (from £3,000). The prime minister presented this as a way of empowering students, explaining 'instead of government deciding where the money goes, students will. The spending power is directly in their hands. That gives students the greatest possible influence over the service they receive – and puts real pressure on universities to drive up standards' (Cameron, 2010c). The idea is that universities will be forced to become more competitive and work harder to attract students since their funding is to come directly from their fees rather than from government now that the annual block grant to underwrite teaching has been virtually abolished. It is unlikely, however, that students feel genuinely empowered, saddled with huge sums of debt to be paid off later in life. Universities themselves have certainly not been empowered as, like schools, they are forced to comply with the disciplines of the market and are subject to a significant amount of government interference over their research agendas (Head, 2011). The bureaucratic demands of the Research Assessment Exercise (which since 1986 has evaluated research produced by English universities to determine the level of funding they should be allocated)

DOI: 10.1057/9781137505781.0005

continue and the immense pressure to attract external funding has been exacerbated by the most recent reforms. The risk of researchers being co-opted and tailoring their research agendas to external requirements is significant. Indeed, a government funding body, the Arts and Humanities Research Council, on the government's insistence, reportedly placed great pressure on academics receiving its funding to prioritise research on the 'Big Society' (Boffey, 2011). The irony of this was not lost on McAnulla, 'given the Big Society's emphasis on facilitating creativity free from state regulation' (ibid., p. 178).

In health, patients were to be given 'more control and doctors more professional freedom' (Cameron, 2011a). The discourse of freedom, empowerment and localism was also evident here. One government white paper paving the way for reform was even titled 'Equity and Excellence: Liberating the NHS' (Department of Health, 2010). The document noted that patients should be empowered, given greater choice, for example, in selecting their GP and the type of treatment they receive. With regard to promoting citizens' health, the coalition favoured 'soft paternalism', eschewing stricter regulation of the food and drink industries and instead encouraging citizens to make the right choices themselves (Page, 2011, p. 96). Lying behind the liberal discourse of empowerment is a desire to further responsibilise individual citizens.

A second health white paper promised to end 'top-down government in healthcare' (ibid., p. 95). Consequently, under the *Health and Social Care Act 2012* Primary Care Trusts, public administrative bodies responsible for purchasing patient care, were replaced by Clinical Commissioning Groups, to be controlled by consortia of GPs (Kober-Smith, 2014). The new bodies were encouraged to engage with both private and charitable organisations. Yet, given the lack of expertise of these organisations, regulation is likely to increase in the long term as government attempts to ensure that healthcare standards are upheld (Page, 2011, p. 98). Indeed, a brand new regulator, Monitor, was created to supervise the new market in healthcare. It is also intended to ensure that there is a level playing field between private and charitable providers, but this is a virtually impossible goal to attain, given the superior tendering expertise and resources of private companies (TUC, 2011, 176). Between April 2013 and August 2014, 33 per cent of contracts awarded by Clinical Commissioning Groups went to the private sector (BBC, 2014a). As with education reform, it is private companies who seem to be empowered to the detriment of private citizens. As Walker has commented, for local

DOI: 10.1057/9781137505781.0005

communities, 'running' schools and hospitals often amounts to 'no more than being allowed vignettes of scrutiny of what powerful executive managers are up to' (Walker, 2012, p. 16).

What of the *Localism Act 2011*? Has it fared any better in terms of engineering 'a substantial and lasting shift in power away from central government and towards local people', as the government promised (Clarke, 2011, p. 1)? The law officially aimed to provide 'new freedoms and flexibilities for local government' (Department for Communities and Local Government, 2011, p. 4). Consequently, local authorities were given 'a general power of competence', enabling them to do anything an individual can legally do, such as establishing new services and partnerships without having to first seek the approval of central government. Yet, the power is somewhat limited in scope due to continued government regulation and budgetary pressures: the government retains the right to amend the primary legislation; it has placed limits on the number of company structures that can be created by councils; and it has declared that charges can only be made for discretionary services which recover costs (Keeling, 2013). Local authorities also face the challenge of significant cuts to central government funding. The 2010 Spending Review planned to reduce local authority funding (except for schools, police and fire services) by 14 per cent between April 2011 and March 2015 (NAO, 2013a, p. 13). In a report released early in 2013, the National Audit Office found that this had resulted in some services, notably library services, being reduced or cut altogether (ibid., pp. 23–4).

Councils have the power to raise local taxes – their main source of funding after central government grants – but in practice central government has set a cap above which taxes cannot be raised without first holding a local referendum to approve the decision. It even introduced incentives for councils not to raise local taxes (ibid., p. 18). At the same time, councils were encouraged to offer businesses reductions to rates – the third main source of local government funding – ostensibly to encourage increased investment. Cutting costs seems to have been a central driver of government policy here: the government's guide to the *Localism Act* explained that the general power of competence would give 'councils more freedom to work together with others in new ways to drive down cost' (Department for Communities and Local Government, 2011, p. 4). In such a difficult financial climate, the overall effect of the coalition's localism agenda, with regard to local government at least, was to provide the responsibility without the power (Pipe, 2013).

DOI: 10.1057/9781137505781.0005

With regard to local communities, the *Localism Act* gave voluntary or community bodies, charities, parish councils and two or more local authority employees the 'right to express an interest' in running local services in place of local authorities. The so-called 'community right to challenge' enables them to make a formal bid. Local authorities are obliged to consider how the proposal may improve the economic, social and environmental well-being of the relevant area (following the enactment of the *Social Value Act 2012*). Projects may be funded by central government grants. It is difficult to assess whether or not this initiative has resulted in genuine community empowerment since, according to the Secretary of State for Communities and Local Government, the government does not collate information relating to how many times the Community Right to Challenge has been used since it came into force on 27 June 2012 or regarding the success of these challenges (Williams, 2014). Given that local councils are under no obligation to accept the community challenge to the current provider of services, it may be supposed that the power of the local community remains subservient to that of local authorities.

Under the *Localism Act*, parish councils and community groups also have a new 'right to bid' to buy over buildings or services of community value that risk being closed or sold off to the private sector (see Sandford, 2013). A number of local pubs have been recognised as assets of community value by local councils, meaning that local communities must be informed if they are being sold off, giving them a chance to make a bid to buy. The law does not give the right of first refusal to local communities – they can simply enter the bidding process along with other interested parties – although once a building or service is recognised as a community asset, the sale is stalled to enable the community to put together a bid and to apply for funding via new grants from organisations such as the private sector Social Investment Business Group. Communities wishing to present such a bid face a number of hurdles. First, they have to convince the local council to determine whether or not a building or service should be considered as a community asset, capable of furthering 'the social wellbeing or social interests of the local community' (*Social Value Act 2012*). Not all buildings have the potential to become community assets as certain types of land are exempt from the law, notably residential property. It is also up to the council to define who exactly may be considered as a 'community interest group' capable of putting a bid forward. Perhaps most significantly, it is very difficult for

DOI: 10.1057/9781137505781.0005

community groups to compete on the open market, especially given the rising price of property in many areas in England (Blunden, 2012).

The *Localism Act* also aimed to involve communities in local planning decisions. Lamenting the fact that the previous planning system 'did not give members of the public enough influence over decisions that make a big difference to their lives' (Department for Communities and Local Government, 2011, p. 11), the government introduced a new right for communities to draw up 'neighbourhood plans' regarding future development in their area. These plans are worked out in 'neighbourhood forums' whereby communities and local authorities get together to discuss planning issues. Once a plan is finalised, it is inspected independently before being put to a local referendum. If approved, the local authority is obliged to adopt it. Yet, these rights are also somewhat limited. Plans must conform to national planning policy and local development plans drawn up by local authorities. This means that the new law cannot be used by local residents to block development which they consider to be detrimental to the area – they merely allow them to 'shape and influence where that development will go and what it will look like' (Smith, 2014, p. 3). Indeed, they will continue to have no right of appeal against local planning decisions – these may only be referred for judicial review. Furthermore, the powers of central government remain significant, with the Secretary of State holding the right to 'recover' a planning appeal, in other words to examine an appeal against a local authority's decision to reject a planning application and to personally take the final decision (ibid., p. 3). Furthermore, the *Growth and Infrastructure Act 2013* (section 1) notably allows local authorities who are deemed not to be handling planning applications quickly enough to be bypassed by developers who may make applications directly to the Secretary of State.

A final key change introduced by the *Localism Act* was to allow 'more decisions about housing [to be] taken locally' (Department for Communities and Local Government, 2011, p. 11). This measure was essentially intended to empower local authorities, 'freeing them' of the obligation to grant lifetime tenancies and allowing them to force homeless people into accepting accommodation in the private rented sector (rather than giving them the choice of moving into temporary accommodation until a long-term social home becomes available). There is no longer any obligation on the part of local authorities to provide long-term social housing. We do not know how many households are currently housed by local authorities in the private rented sector – as the minister for Communities and Local Government explained in answer to a Commons question on the subject, 'this information is not held centrally' (Hopkins, 2014). Yet the new policy certainly appears to favour private landlords to the detriment of local communities.

In general, private sector interests have been protected or even furthered by the coalition's 'Big Society'/localism agenda. In education and healthcare, the private sector has been allowed to extend its reach and benefit from new markets; under the *Localism Act*, local authorities have been encouraged to provide 'clients' for the private rented sector and to ensure that its interests are protected when it comes to planning and development. Meanwhile, the powers that have been granted to local communities have remained limited. Yet, if local communities are to be able to compete with private companies for the running and provision of local services, they will need to be given much greater powers. As things stand, the playing field is far from level. As Crowe has suggested, there is a 'mismatch between the bold claims of a radical decentralisation of power and the raft of relatively small proposals which it is claimed will achieve it' (2011, p. 656).

As suggested earlier, we can better understand the coalition's localism agenda by regarding it as a technique of governmentality. Under the localism agenda, the coalition has interpreted empowerment as responsibility: parents are to accept responsibility for their children's education, taking the initiative to get involved in the setting up of new schools; patients are to be responsible for choosing which treatment or healthcare service is best for them; local authorities are to accept responsibility for driving down costs and efficiently managing local budgets; local communities should take responsibility for planning policy in their local areas and bid to manage local services and save them from closure. As David Cameron himself said, the main aim of the Big Society was to foster a 'culture of responsibility' (2010d). Yet, as we have seen, this responsibility comes without real power, preventing it from delivering effective freedom. If freedom is reinforced, this is a 'by-product' rather than its immediate aim (Edwards, 2012, p. 100). The main aim seems to have been to offload State responsibility for public services while seeking to place this in the hands of local communities.

This is not just a smokescreen for privatisation, even if the private sector is set to be the main beneficiary of the policy. It is about governing more effectively. Even if local communities are not genuinely empowered, the discourse of localism at least makes them appear to be

DOI: 10.1057/9781137505781.0005

more responsible for fixing the social problems associated with 'broken society'. The government can claim to have given them a range of tools to improve their local schools and get involved in local democracy, for example. This is presented as preferable to solutions imposed from central government. Who could be opposed to getting local communities involved in repairing the 'broken society' – surely social problems need 'social' solutions, developed by and for local communities? This would seem to be a truly democratic form of politics. Yet, in a democracy it is expected that government should take responsibility when things go wrong – this is the most basic notion of the social contract. But increased community responsibility goes hand-in-hand with decreased government responsibility. Government constantly states that its powers are limited, that it cannot provide magic solutions to social problems, especially in the current economic crisis. As Cameron declared:

> The old top-down, big-government approach has failed in Britain, and even if you believed in it, even if you still believe in it, there isn't really any government money left to try it with. Gordon spent it all. It's all gone. So we need something different, and that is where our big idea comes in. (2010d)

State-centred solutions are seen to be entirely ineffective and, even if government wanted to apply them, it could not do so owing to budgetary constraints. Such discourse effectively deresponsibilises central government. This strategy is sometimes referred to as one of 'depoliticisation' whereby government seeks to take the political heat out of certain issues by claiming that there is not a great deal it can do about them. It justifies a rolling back of the state yet, as Foster et al. point out, there is simultaneously a rolling forward since government control is not relinquished (2014). On the contrary, it is strengthened. As the limited practice of localism so far has shown, the State retains an important directive and regulatory role, preventing citizens from becoming truly empowered. The State has not been decentred under the coalition and local communities have not been empowered. The following chapter will seek to determine whether or not individuals have been empowered in the 'Big Society'.

DOI: 10.1057/9781137505781.0005

2
Empowering the People

Abstract: *This chapter focuses on the Coalition's efforts to responsibilise specific 'problematic' groups of people. It is argued that a form of moral authoritarianism permeates policy in this area, whereby subjects can only be 'made' free via a number of coercive policies which seek to render them more responsible. Policy towards the poor, immigrants and ethnic minorities is analysed and it is argued that coercion is regarded as the only route to becoming 'empowered' fully fledged citizens. While policies towards the poor and immigrants are underpinned by moral authoritarianism, the Coalition has nonetheless shown itself to be morally liberal with regard to homosexuals, allowing it to present a more acceptable 'modern' image of itself and to mask the illiberalism deployed with regard to other populations.*

Keywords: immigration; moral authoritarianism; muscular liberalism; welfare

Bell, Emma. *Soft Power and Freedom under the Coalition: State-Corporate Power and the Threat to Democracy.* Basingstoke: Palgrave Macmillan, 2015. DOI: 10.1057/9781137505781.0006.

The decentralisation of power from the central state was not just intended to benefit local authorities and communities: the 'radical redistribution of power' was intended to be in favour of 'councils, communities *and homes* across the nation' (HM Government, 2010a, p. 7, *my italics*). Individuals and families were therefore encouraged to get involved in the 'Big Society' project, not just as volunteers helping out in the running and delivery of local services such as schools, but also as responsible citizens, taking charge of their own problems in order to repair the 'broken society'. For the Conservative Party in particular, this entailed taking a new interest in social problems, with Cameron promising that under his leadership, the party would be 'as radical in social reform as Margaret Thatcher was in economic reform' (Cameron, 2008). Indeed, in order to differentiate the party from the Thatcher era, widely regarded as having nurtured a politics of indifference towards social problems, it was important for the Conservatives to go beyond a concern with economics alone. The Conservative approach under Cameron was in many ways radically different from that of the Thatcher era. Most notably, for the first time, the party recognised the existence of relative poverty, accepting the definition as 60 per cent of the median income (Willetts, 2005). In recognition that the Conservative Party should be concerned about social issues, the Centre for Social Justice was established in 2004 by Iain Duncan Smith, former Conservative Party leader, to conduct research into social breakdown in Britain. Its policy recommendations were highly influential on the development of Conservative Party policy under David Cameron. Together with other centre-right think tanks such as Policy Exchange, it helped to put flesh on the idea of 'compassionate conservatism'. Starting from the belief that we share an interconnectedness with other people as members of society, the philosophy argues that we are capable of sympathy for other people's problems and ought to feel concerned by them (Norman & Ganesh, 2006). But ultimately, it is for the individual to assume responsibility for these problems (ibid.). Since State interventions are regarded as necessarily coercive, they should be eschewed in favour of promoting freedom, the necessary correlative of which is the assumption of individual responsibility (ibid., p. 61).

Such ideas could easily find sympathy with the Liberal Democrats given their long commitment to social liberalism which entails promoting social justice without impinging upon individual freedom. Yet, while Asquith's New Liberals of the early twentieth century regarded limited state interventionism as necessary to realise liberal ideals by removing

DOI: 10.1057/9781137505781.0006

the barriers to freedom created by poverty, contemporary 'Orange Book' liberals share a concern with the Conservatives about 'nanny state liberalism' which may undermine individual freedom (Laws, 2012, p. 32). In government (if not among the party grassroots), there was a broad policy consensus, both parties sharing a commitment to tackle social problems via the promotion of individual responsibility (Driver, 2011, p. 106). They agreed that it was necessary to abandon 'top-down' approaches, making the promotion of individual responsibility the chief aim of the welfare system (HM Government, 2010a, p. 23). Yet, as this chapter seeks to demonstrate, this apparently liberal policy was tainted by a strain of illiberalism as extremely coercive measures were adopted to enforce individual responsibility. Liberal discourse was sometimes underpinned by a discourse of moral authoritarianism. The poor in particular were the focus of these policies but other groups, notably migrants and ethnic minorities, also felt the brunt of illiberal measures intended to empower them. Simultaneously, however, the Coalition also showed itself capable of social liberalism with regard to certain groups it regarded as being sufficiently empowered and responsible.

Empowerment through welfare reform

The coalition government considered the welfare system it inherited as an impediment to freedom and as incapable of solving social problems. Rather like Margaret Thatcher or Tony Blair before him, Cameron believed that the system 'trapped people in poverty' by creating 'perverse incentives' whereby it was possible to be better off living on benefits than working (Cameron, 2012a). Indeed, Chancellor George Osborne declared that claiming benefits is 'a lifestyle choice' (2010a). The solution then was to reform the welfare system to ensure that people would be given the opportunity to become independent. This is what drives a 'compassionate' approach to welfare. As Cameron declared in 2012, justifying further reforms to welfare, 'compassion isn't measured out in benefit cheques – it's in the chances you give people...the chance to get a job, to get on, to get that sense of achievement that only comes from doing a hard day's work for a proper day's pay' (2012a). In short, 'compassion' entails helping people to accept responsibility.

Another way in which welfare claimants were to be 'set free' was to encourage private and voluntary sector partners to administer the welfare

DOI: 10.1057/9781137505781.0006

system, with non-state agencies being presented as less coercive and therefore more legitimate than those of the State. As the Conservative intellectual Oliver Letwin suggested, 'When an authority visits the home it is an authority. When a voluntary agency funded by the State visits the home it is a helping hand' (2002a).

The first of these methods to empower individuals, setting them free from welfare dependency, was to translate into reforms increasing conditionality in the welfare system. The flagship policy here was the Work Programme, the new welfare-to-work programme introduced in June 2011 to replace all existing New Deal schemes introduced under New Labour. Participation in the programme is compulsory for all unemployed people aged 25 or over who have been claiming unemployment benefit for 12 months or more (young people aged 18–24 must participate if they have been claiming for 9 months or more). It should be noted that current unemployment benefit, known as 'jobseeker's allowance' is gradually being replaced by the Universal Credit. The new benefit was first introduced in October 2013 and will gradually be introduced nationally by 2017. Under the Work Programme, claimants will be referred to government-approved service providers, mostly private companies, who are responsible for helping them back into work. As part of the government's policy regarding decentralisation, these providers are given considerable freedom over the kind of support and services they offer. Formal agreements are drawn up between service providers and claimants and the latter obliged to fulfil their obligations under their 'claimant commitment'. The former are meant to be paid according to the results they deliver even if this principle has not been strictly enforced. According to a report by the National Audit Office, the Department for Work and Pensions 'may be paying contractors for performance they are not actually achieving' largely due to invalid claims for 'sustainment payments' (money paid to contractors when people remain in work for more than six months). It estimated that the Department has already incurred losses amounting to £11 million by March 2014 and was set to lose a further £25 million should no changes be made (NAO, 2014).

As under the New Labour New Deal schemes, claimants risk losing benefits if they do not comply. Yet, the government-designed sanctions scheme is much stricter than before. Under the new scheme relating to unemployment benefits introduced in October 2012, 'high level sanctions' can be imposed (e.g., on claimants who leave a job voluntarily) withdrawing payment for 13 weeks for a first offence, rising to 52 weeks

DOI: 10.1057/9781137505781.0006

for a third offence or more. It was estimated that the total amount of money withheld as a result of benefit sanctions rose from £11 million in 2009–10 to £60 million in 2012–13 (Timms, 2014), prompting much concern about the extent to which the sanctions have been used.

Tough sanctions also apply to those placed on the Mandatory Work Activity Scheme. This programme is primarily aimed at the low-skilled who may have most difficulty finding work. Claimants must engage in 'work-related activity' for up to 30 hours per week over a four-week period. Should they fail to take part in the scheme without a very good reason, strict benefit sanctions apply. The scheme may entail claimants working for the benefit of the community, carrying out park maintenance or working in charity shops, for example. A number of charities have boycotted the scheme, criticising it for introducing 'forced volunteers' (Malik, 2013). Despite criticisms, the scheme was extended under the 'Help to Work Programme' introduced in spring 2014. The programme, specifically targeted at those who have been claiming unemployment benefit for two years or more, may oblige claimants to attend daily meetings with jobcentre advisers, place them on an education or training placement, or force them to participate in a mandatory work activity for up to six months.

On top of these disincentives to claim welfare, incentives to work were to be added. The principal means of doing so was through the introduction of the universal credit under the *Welfare Reform Act 2012*. At the time of writing in autumn 2014, the new credit is in the process of being rolled out and is due to be fully implemented by 2017. The scheme was originally proposed by the Centre for Social Justice in a report titled *Dynamic Benefits: Towards Welfare That Works* (Centre for Social Justice, 2009). It was intended to tackle what the report described as disincentives to work, notably created by the working tax credits originally introduced under New Labour. The report highlights the fact that many families risked losing their credits once they went beyond certain thresholds, effectively penalising them for wanting to work longer hours (ibid., pp. 97–9). Under the Universal Credit, tax credits and benefits are merged under a single system and the former will generally be withdrawn at a lower rate than previously once people start to work more. Yet, given the way the system is set to operate, lone parents may find themselves worse off while couples, especially with children, may be the main beneficiaries (Brewer et al., 2012). As a result, the new system will not 'make work pay' for all, meaning that not everyone will be 'freed' from benefit traps.

DOI: 10.1057/9781137505781.0006

Furthermore, as Mabbett points out, the system actually has the capacity to be highly coercive:

> It has the potential to change the level of compulsion and administrative control significantly. People who are working while also receiving income from the state will be caught in the administrative and supervisory net of the benefit system. They will be expected to increase their hours and earnings if the benefits office deems that suitable opportunities are available. Universal Credit is a highly illiberal reform. It reinstates coercion for many households which had found their own ways through the labour market and the benefit system. (Mabbett, 2013, p. 45)

The second way in which welfare claimants were to be 'set free' was even less effective. The idea was that individuals would be empowered by involving non-state actors in the provision of welfare services. As Cameron declared:

> We are making welfare much more responsive to individual needs. We're sweeping away all the old top down centralised bureaucracy that treated people like numbers in a machine. And in its place, we're saying to the person who is unemployed and desperate to get a job – we will make sure you get the personalised help you want. We will give each of you a proper assessment of your needs. And then, through the Work Programme, we'll invite our best social enterprises, charities and businesses to come into the welfare system and give you intensive, personal assistance to find work. (2011b)

In practice, of the 40 government contracts established under the Work Programme, 35 were awarded to private sector companies and just 3 to third sector organisations. The contracts operate under a 'black box' model, meaning that service providers are relatively free to determine what services they will offer to the unemployed. The idea is that they will be incentivised to innovate, especially since they are paid according to the results they achieve, measured as the number of people they may get back into the workplace. The government presumably hopes that this will provide such companies with incentives to provide good-quality services. Yet, it ignores the possible disincentives such a system may create with regard to the most 'difficult' jobseekers. Indeed, researchers have found that private companies contracted under the Work Programme are commonly engaged in practices of 'creaming' and 'parking'. The former practice refers to when providers pick the 'best clients', namely those who will be the easiest to get back onto the labour market, while 'parking' the most hard-to-reach, in other words leaving those who present

DOI: 10.1057/9781137505781.0006

more of a challenge to get back into work to depend on benefits (Rees et al., 2013, pp. 6–8). This is despite the Department for Work and Pensions' efforts to provide greater financial incentives to private companies with regard to these harder-to-reach groups. The outcome is that disabled people and lone parents in particular have much lower chances of getting back into the labour market compared to other groups. Indeed, a report by the National Audit Office suggests that the performance of the Work Programme overall with regard to both easier- and harder-to-help groups is very similar to that of previous welfare-to-work schemes (NAO, 2013a, pp. 21–36). This suggests that many unemployed people, but particularly those who are furthest removed from the labour market, remain 'trapped' on benefits.

The government's welfare reform programme would thus not appear to be particularly effective on its own terms. If the overall unemployment rate decreased under the Coalition to reach a five-year low of 6.6 per cent of the economically active population in June 2014 (ONS, 2014a), the link with the Work Programme is hard to establish. The latter may simply serve to mask the real numbers of people without work as those engaged in unpaid work schemes under the programme are not counted on the official unemployment register (Ball, 2013). It could also be said that the welfare reform programme has not been particularly successful in terms of empowerment on account of the failure of work to truly set people free from poverty and on account of the degree of coercion employed to attempt to force people off benefits.

Trapped in poverty

The government makes the false assumption that work automatically equates with empowerment: work is seen as the main route for giving people 'greater control over their lives' (Smith, 2014). Despite its promise to 'make work pay', for many people it is low-paid work, not welfare, that traps them in poverty and prevents them from having such effective control over their lives. Indeed, more than half (6.7 million people) of the 13 million people living in poverty in the United Kingdom live in households in which at least one person is in work (MacInnes et al., 2013, p. 26). The minimum wage, introduced by Blair's first New Labour government in 1998, has done nothing to prevent this upward trend, especially as the minimum wage has continued to decline in real terms

DOI: 10.1057/9781137505781.0006

under the Coalition (Low Pay Commission, 2014, pp. 179–81). Working extra hours would make no difference to families living in poverty where at least one earner is paid below the 'living wage' (defined as the amount an individual needs to earn to cover the basic costs of living) since in 40 per cent of these households all the adults already work full-time (MacInnes et al., 2013, p. 48). In addition, on account of the reductions in help with childcare costs introduced under Universal Credit, some parents in low-paid work will find that they are worse off if they work full-time (Hirsch & Hartfree, 2013). Furthermore, working families are expected to be severely hit by cuts to benefits. For example, 20 per cent of those who face increased payments as a result of the replacement of Council Tax Benefit by Council Tax Support are working families (MacInnes et al., 2013, p. 26). Under the old system, these rates were fixed by central government to ensure that the very poorest households would be exempt from council tax. Local councils may now fix their own rates of discounts. Many working households are also affected by the government's decision to cap housing benefit at £500 for families (£350 for single people) as of April 2013 despite the fact that those entitled to working tax credits are exempt from the cap in order not to discourage people from working extra hours. Research has shown that an ever-growing proportion of working households are in need of housing benefit, suggesting that many will be affected by the cap (London Councils, 2013, p. 13). Iain Duncan Smith, the Secretary of State for Work and Pensions, has presented the cap as a way of empowering individuals. Speaking of the old system, he declared:

> It has not been fair on benefit recipients themselves. How many of us here would want to live trapped in a system where it was more worthwhile sitting on benefits than going to work? Now, having capped the amount paid to some 30,000 households, these families face the same choices about where they live and what they can afford as everyone else. (2014)

Yet, in reality, the reform has been experienced as highly coercive as many people find their choices about where to live are severely restricted as they are forced to search for alternative cheaper accommodation, often far from their place of work, family and friends, in order to avoid being penalised under the cap. This is particularly the case in London and the south-east where rents are extremely high.

People may also be disempowered in the workplace itself by the limitation of their employment rights. The *Enterprise and Regulatory Reform*

DOI: 10.1057/9781137505781.0006

Act 2013 implemented changes to the employment tribunal system by which employees may claim redress and enforce their rights at work. Far from empowering employees, employers were to be freed of 'red tape' by promoting settlement agreements and thus limiting the number of cases actually reaching tribunals (Scott & Williams, 2014, p. 151). Section 69 of the Act removes the civil liability of employers when health and safety regulations are breached, meaning that employees who suffer accidents at work will generally have to prove negligence on the part of the employer if they wish to obtain compensation. Employers were also freed from much government regulation of employment relations. The Coalition favoured a voluntary approach by employers, enabling them for example to choose whether or not to introduce flexible working hours or to pay a 'living wage' (ibid., p. 153). This effectively enabled government to divest itself of responsibility for the implementation of such policies without necessarily reinforcing the responsibility of employers. While it is too early to measure the impact of this legislation on the ground (it only entered into force in October 2013), it is striking how this soft-touch approach to employers contrasts starkly with the coercive approach adopted towards employees and benefit claimants.

Muscular liberalism and welfare

The coalition government's welfare reforms in practice go far beyond reinforcing conditionality. Often they entail outright coercion of benefit claimants. Claimants are not empowered, least of all through low-paid work. In many cases they are rendered quite powerless and have little means of redress against the sanctions that may be applied to them should they fail to accept the stringent conditions of their jobseekers agreements: under the *Legal Aid, Sentencing and Punishment of Offenders Act 2012*, most welfare benefit cases are deemed ineligible for legal aid. As with the public service reforms discussed in Chapter 1, the role of the State remains significant even where responsibility has been off-loaded onto private and voluntary-sector agencies. As Driver commented even before the Coalition came to power, 'for all the talk of rolling out society, there remains a significant role for the State as agent of social reform in Cameron Conservatism' (Driver, 2009, p. 94). It is indeed the State that has engineered these reforms and that applies sanctions to ensure that they are effective.

DOI: 10.1057/9781137505781.0006

Rather than 'compassionate conservatism', the Coalition's approach may more appropriately be described as one of 'muscular liberalism'. Although the phrase was originally used by both Cameron and Clegg in relation to government policy towards multiculturalism, it could certainly be applied to welfare reform. Cameron defined 'muscular liberalism' in the following terms:

> Frankly, we need a lot less of the passive tolerance of recent years and a much more active, muscular liberalism. A passively tolerant society says to its citizens, as long as you obey the law we will just leave you alone. It stands neutral between different values. But I believe a genuinely liberal country does much more; it believes in certain values and actively promotes them. (Cameron, 2011c)

The coalition government certainly attempted to actively promote the 'liberal' values of hard work, independence and personal responsibility, through coercive means if necessary. Underpinning such a strategy was a strong sense of moral authoritarianism that pitted these 'liberal' values against the supposedly defective values of benefits claimants. The problems faced by the latter were presented as a direct result of their values. Indeed, claiming out-of-work welfare benefits was one of the six criteria identified by the Centre for Social Justice in identifying 'troubled families' who were in need of state intervention to 'turn their lives around'. For David Willetts, poverty is not just about money but also about values (Willetts, 2005). For Iain Duncan Smith, it is necessary to tackle the 'culture of worklessness' (2014).

There is in reality no evidence of such a culture in Britain today: most claimants see social, psychological and material value in paid work (Shildrick et al., 2012, pp. 22–8); only 17 per cent of households were workless in 2013 and just 1.5 per cent of all households contained members who had never worked (MacInnes et al., 2013, p. 42). Yet the idea that claimants possess different values from the rest of society serves as an important rhetorical device to promote the value of work. Clear distinctions are therefore made between the 'workers' and the 'shirkers'. Chancellor George Osborne painted a vivid picture of the difference between these two groups of people in his party conference speech of 2012, asking 'Where is the fairness, we ask, for the shift-worker, leaving home in the dark hours of the early morning, who looks up at the closed blinds of their next door neighbour sleeping off a life on benefits?' (2012). Nick Clegg was more careful with his rhetoric, avoiding direct criticism

DOI: 10.1057/9781137505781.0006

of benefit claimants. He described those who 'want to get up and get on' as belonging to 'alarm clock Britain', comparing them to the wealthy who have no need to work hard to make ends meet, but his message was the same: 'We are on the side of people who work hard' (implying that there are many people who do not work hard and who are unwilling to do so) (2011a). Such discourse was reminiscent of that of Tony Blair who claimed that welfare claimants often belong to an underclass set apart from the rest of society by its unique set of values and culture which differ from the mainstream (1997).

For the coalition government, some benefits claimants, however, were thought of as deserving, notably pensioners. Unlike the rate of benefits which is now indexed to the lower consumer price index ensuring that its real value has decreased, the rate of the state pension increases in line with earnings, prices or 2.5 per cent, whichever is greatest. Yet, there is also a certain degree of soft coercion present in the pensions system as citizens are now automatically enrolled on private pension schemes, whether they choose to subscribe to such a policy or not (Mabbett, 2013). Both pensioners and working-age welfare claimants are to be made 'responsible'; the former by gentle nudging and the latter by more blatant coercion. In both cases, the aim is to bring about a cultural change whereby neither group depends on the State for subsistence but rather on private companies.

This attempt to create responsible, independent citizens through cultural change may be regarded as being somewhat similar to the creation of a *vitalpolitik*. This idea was put forward by the ordoliberal intellectual Alexander Rüstow in the 1930s. For the ordoliberals, the market could only be free if government intervened to secure the conditions of free enterprise by guaranteeing a legal, social and moral order (Bonefeld, 2013). Social policy should be primarily directed at effecting cultural and moral change to ensure that workers are content to participate in the free market. It should work to create *vitalpolitik*, in other words a politics capable of ensuring the vitality of an entrepreneurial society. It is not the material welfare of workers that counts but rather their capacity to accept risks and to act responsibly to prepare for them. For the ordoliberals, such a change could be effected by 'soft' means, turning workers into private property owners with a stake in the system. As Bonefeld puts it, 'Vitalpolitik is to transform a proletarian mentality into the moral sentiments of private property, harnessing workers as self-responsible entrepreneurs of their own labour power' (ibid., p. 118). Such thinking

DOI: 10.1057/9781137505781.0006

was mirrored in Thatcher's desire to create a 'property-owning democracy' and in the current coalition government's attempts to extend home ownership under its own right-to-buy scheme (although the ordoliberals would not have approved of people financing ownership through debt). Such 'soft' means of effecting cultural change did not exclude coercion, especially since the ordoliberals had a very limited conception of freedom, one that was limited to 'the freedom of the self-responsible entrepreneur' (ibid., p. 119). The same could be said to be true of the coalition government. We shall return to this discussion in Chapter 6.

Dean has described contemporary attempts, dating from the Thatcher period onwards, to create responsible, independent citizens as forming part of a 'post-welfarist regime of the social' (Dean, 2010). By this he means that the State no longer fulfils its social responsibilities in the way that it did under the postwar Keynesian welfare state. As the distinction between public and private has become blurred in neoliberal society, the market and a range of new agencies come to fulfil functions previously assumed exclusively by the State. Services are to be coordinated by market rather than bureaucratic means. It is through the market that individuals can exercise real freedom, learning to make choices for themselves. Non-state agencies are meant to be our partners and facilitators, helping us to take responsibility for our own lives and manage the risks that the State previously sought to protect us from. If this means less state intervention, it does not however mean less government in the sense that individuals are now controlled by a wider range of state agencies. Indeed, rather than the coalition government reducing its power over individuals, it may be argued that it has augmented it by diffusing it through the non-state actors of the 'Big Society'. Individuals are coerced by a range of different actors into becoming 'responsible' and independent from state social provision. This is 'muscular liberalism' in action.

Muscular liberalism and multiculturalism

British citizens are not the only people to be subjected to muscular liberalism. Of course, as highlighted above, the term was originally used by David Cameron in the context of the multiculturalism debate (Cameron, 2011c). Migrants and ethnic minorities are seen to be particularly in need of coercive interventions to make them accept 'liberal' values for two main reasons. First, migrants are often presented as lacking responsibility

DOI: 10.1057/9781137505781.0006

and being dependent on state help. David Cameron himself declared that people are right to be concerned that 'some people might be able to come and take advantage of our generosity without making a proper contribution to our country' and promised to reform the system to ensure that people come to Britain 'for the right reasons' and are not 'drawn by the attractiveness of our benefits system' (2013a). Secondly, some groups of migrants and ethnic minorities are thought to harbour 'real hostility towards Western democracy and liberal values', such as respect for gender equality (Cameron, 2011c).

The argument that migrants as a group are attracted by Britain's 'generous' benefit system is unproven. A report for the European Commission found that the majority of migrants within the European Union move to find or take up employment (ICF GHK/Milieu, 2013). Overall, the majority of migrants come to the United Kingdom to study (36 per cent), to take up a job (23 per cent) or to look for a job (13 per cent) (Vargas-Silva, 2014). Even if it could be proved that migrants as a whole choose to come to Britain because of its 'generous' benefits system, this would be a decision informed by ignorance on the part of migrants given that the European Committee of Social Rights considers that Britain's welfare system is 'manifestly inadequate' and in breach of the European Social Charter (2014; 17–19). Furthermore, it is rather simplistic to suggest that the welfare system alone is a key driver of immigration since so many other factors also play a role in migration decisions, notably wage and income differentials between countries of origin and destination, colonial links and networks and migration policies in countries of destination (Czaikia & De Haas, 2013). The idea that migrants come to Britain to claim benefits, implies that they live on benefits when they stay. This claim is also spurious. EU nationals are actually more likely to be in employment than nationals living in the same country (ICF GHK/Milieu, 2013). Migrants as a whole, whether they come from within or outside the European Union, make a positive contribution to the UK fiscal system. A recent report found that migrants arriving in the United Kingdom since 2000 'contributed far more in taxes than they received in benefits' (Dustmann & Frattini, 2013, p. 28). Indeed, these migrants were found to be 45 per cent less likely than native Britons to receive state benefits or tax credits (ibid., p. 28).

Despite the evidence, the government continues to perpetuate such myths about immigration, justifying the further limitation of access to benefits for migrants. For example, David Cameron is currently

DOI: 10.1057/9781137505781.0006

attempting to curtail the benefit rights of EU citizens living in the United Kingdom. All EU member states must provide the same benefit rights to citizens from other EU countries as they provide to their own citizens. EU citizens simply have to prove that they are 'habitually resident' in a member state in order to claim benefits. The United Kingdom, however, introduced a stricter 'right-to-reside' test in 2008, forcing EU citizens to prove that they are 'actively seeking work' before they may claim benefits. This rule is currently being challenged by the European Commission but David Cameron attempted to make the rule even stricter. As of November 2014 EU migrants have only been able to claim unemployment benefits for a maximum of three months. Furthermore, Cameron publicly declared support for German proposals to return jobless EU-nationals to their country of origin if they fail to find work after a certain period of time, regardless of whether or not they are 'actively seeking work' (Watt, 2014).

For migrants coming to Britain from outside the European Union, the coalition government placed a cap on net migration in an attempt to reduce it 'from hundreds of thousands a year, to just tens of thousands' (Cameron, 2013a). The government has not so far succeeded, net migration standing at 212,000 in the year ending December 2013 (ONS, 2014b). Yet, a number of new restrictions have been placed on immigration in an attempt to reach the target of fewer than 100,000 new migrants per year. Stricter citizenship and language tests have been introduced. Student visas are now only granted to those who show a high level of English language proficiency and have adequate funds to be self-sufficient while in Britain. It has also become more difficult for families of those non-EU nationals already settled in the United Kingdom to come to Britain. For example, since July 2012, UK citizens or settled foreign nationals wishing to sponsor their partner or spouse to join them in the United Kingdom must prove that they have a minimum gross annual income of £18,600. Henceforth, only those people who are considered to be economically useful and self-sufficient will be welcome in the United Kingdom. The system is increasingly based on the market value of migrants rather than on their need to enter the country. As Cameron declared, the new immigration rules mean 'ensuring that those who do come here are the brightest and the best, the people we really need, with the skills and entrepreneurial talent to help create the British jobs and growth that will help us to win in the global race' (2013a). As with British nationals, strict rules are justified in the aim of creating responsible, economically independent citizens. It

DOI: 10.1057/9781137505781.0006

is hoped that these citizens, who are integrated in the labour market and who are fluent English-speakers, will have no difficulty participating fully in British society and assimilating British values.

Ethnic minorities already resident in Britain were seen to pose more of a problem for the coalition government. In his now infamous Munich speech on multiculturalism, delivered in early 2011, Cameron expressed concern about the existence of 'segregated communities' in Britain who 'live separate lives, apart from each other and apart from the mainstream', often 'behaving in ways that run completely counter to our values' (2011c). In this analysis it is multiculturalism that is a threat to liberal values and even to the peace and security of the nation (Cameron's decision to use a speech on terrorism and national security to criticise multiculturalism made an implicit link between the two issues). He saw 'muscular' interventions as the best way to defend these values. The old 'hands-off' approach whereby migrants were to be largely left alone to integrate into British society was to be replaced by a more forceful state-led approach to ensure that minorities would assimilate liberal values and thus be steered away from violent extremism. The Coalition's main vehicle for doing so would be the 'Preventing Violent Extremism' strategy (known as *Prevent*) initiated by New Labour in 2006. This strategy was intended to be about 'winning hearts and minds' as part of the government's wider anti-terrorism strategy. Significant funding was provided to local authorities with Muslim populations of five per cent or more, to universities and colleges and even to the Prison Service. Funds were primarily to be used to support community organisations thought to be capable of promoting community cohesion and combating extremism (Thomas, 2010). Yet, given that *Prevent* formed part of a wider counter-terrorism strategy, there was considerable involvement by the police and security services, leading many to suggest that this was simply a covert way of increasing surveillance over Muslim communities (Kundnani, 2009). Indeed, the sharing of information between community workers and the police meant that these communities were more likely than others to come under the radar of the police.

The coalition government updated the *Prevent* strategy, notably addressing these concerns about covert surveillance by separating the integration from the security functions of the programme (HM Government, 2011a). Worried that funding had previously been provided to 'the very extremist organisations that Prevent should have been confronting', it also declared that it would not work with 'extremist organisations that

DOI: 10.1057/9781137505781.0006

oppose our values of universal human rights, equality before the law, democracy and full participation in our society' (HM Government, 2011a, p. 1). Henceforth, it was the security services rather than local authorities that were to decide which community-based groups it would be acceptable to work with (Thomas, 2013). The Coalition's *Prevent* strategy thus runs counter to the discourse of localism, giving central government and security services a significant role in determining what community values are deemed to be acceptable.

Locally led integration projects were not to be abandoned, however. Here, the government adopted a more hands-off approach, leaving locally based private and voluntary organisations to foster an 'integrated society' whereby 'neighbourhoods, families and individuals come together on issues which matter to them' (Department for Communities and Local Government, 2012, p. 2). Yet, the problem of community cohesion continued to be defined as resulting from ethnic minority groups, from those who have different 'cultural attitudes and practices'. The solution was no longer regarded as using the law to give such groups more rights but rather using local communities and local government to enforce the responsibilities of those groups to society (ibid., p. 6). This was essentially a policy for assimilation rather than multiculturalism, encouraging all community members to accept 'mainstream British liberal values' (ibid., p. 9). 'Tolerance' is defined as a key value here, yet essentially the strategy is informed by a lack of tolerance towards values which are not regarded as 'mainstream', 'British' or 'liberal'.

Indeed, the entire debate on multiculturalism has been framed in the language of 'secularism, individualism, gender equality, sexual freedom and freedom of expression' (Kundnani, 2012, p. 156). Far from being regarded as a 'liberal' policy in the sense that Roy Jenkins originally intended when he developed the concept of multiculturalism during his time as Home Secretary under the Labour government of Harold Wilson (1965–7), multiculturalism has come to be regarded as the main threat to liberal values as these are now defined. Policies against multiculturalism cannot thus be regarded as illiberal in themselves. Indeed, they are framed in entirely new terms, no longer based on racial differences but rather on differences of values linked to religion, namely Islam (ibid., pp. 160–1). Restrictions on immigration were framed in similar terms, justified by the need to ensure that those who were coming to the country would be able to fully integrate into the job market and their local communities by speaking the language and having the necessary

DOI: 10.1057/9781137505781.0006

skills. Concerns about immigration were also presented as being largely practical rather than about race or ethnicity. David Cameron, along with a number of other spokespeople for the Conservative Party, highlighted the cost of immigration to the benefits system and to public services (Bale et al., 2011, pp. 403–4). Furthermore, the most draconian aspect of immigration policy inherited from the previous government, namely the detention of children, was ended, helping to give an acceptable face to an immigration policy that was in practice rather illiberal.

Moral liberalism?

Alongside these coercive policies adopted towards benefits claimants, migrants and ethnic minorities, the coalition government developed what would appear to be some genuinely liberal policies towards certain minorities. Under the *Marriage (Same Sex Couples) Act 2013* homosexual couples were finally granted the right to marry. Although this law did not grant equal rights to homosexual and heterosexual couples – for example, the former have weaker pension rights on the death of a spouse and are effectively banned from marrying in the Church of England or of Wales – it did represent a significant advance in the direction of social liberalism (Tatchell, 2013). It may seem surprising that the law was passed under a Conservative-led coalition. It was after all a previous Conservative government that prevented homosexuality from being presented as a normal familial relationship in British schools (under the notorious section 28 of the *Local Government Act 1988*). But it should be noted that 'a significant divide remains in the Conservative Party between social liberals and traditionalists' (Hayton, 2010, p. 492). The 2013 law was essentially supported by the Conservative Party modernisers, the Liberal Democrats and the Labour Party. Indeed, 128 Conservative MPs voted against the Bill and Cameron felt obliged to organise a free-vote on the issue given its degree of sensitivity for many members of his party. Many Conservatives had also opposed the Blair government's repeal of section 28 in 2003 (ibid., p. 494). Cameron himself voted against the full repeal of the law, although he subsequently made a full apology about section 28 in 2009, claiming it was 'offensive to gay people' (Watt, 2009). It could perhaps be said that section 28 also contradicted Cameron's discourse on localism and individualism on account of it implying State-directed interference into the curriculum and issues of private morality.

DOI: 10.1057/9781137505781.0006

Despite the apparent contrast between the moral liberalism shown towards homosexuals and the moral authoritarianism shown towards benefits claimants, the 2013 law may also be regarded as fitting in with overall coalition policy. Indeed, it reflects traditional Conservative support for the institution of marriage. According to Hayton, despite his modernising stance towards homosexuality, Cameron 'remains fundamentally Conservative and consistent with...his predecessors in that he regards marriage as the best model of family life and believes that the State should recognise and promote it in some way' (2010, p. 497). For Richardson, recognising gay marriage was simply a way of encouraging gay people to accept mainstream values (2005). Once in a monogamous relationship, it is assumed that they will act responsibly and manage risks such as those posed by AIDS (Richardson, 2005, p. 522). Marriage of course does not just confer rights but also responsibilities on partners to look after each other. Within a stable married relationship, gay people are more likely to be able to provide financial support for one another, rather than relying on the State (ibid., p. 522).

This is not to suggest that there was no genuine commitment to the promotion of gay rights within the coalition government, simply to argue that there is not quite such a contradiction between the policies adopted towards different groups as it may appear. If there was perhaps no deliberate intention to responsibilise gay people under the 2013 Act, this may nonetheless be regarded as a welcome consequence. Indeed, as this chapter has sought to demonstrate, the principal aim of the coalition government's policies to 'redistribute power' to individuals has been responsibilisation. As with the localism agenda, empowerment has not led to freedom but rather to responsibility. Yet, for the government, the two are simply flipsides of the same coin since one can only be truly free if one is responsible. The role of government is to encourage individuals to be responsible but, to do so, it is to take a step back to empower other agencies and institutions to, in turn, empower individuals. Nonetheless, it retains an important directive role and it is always ready to step in and use its coercive power when necessary, to use the 'muscle' of the State to create truly independent, liberal subjects.

DOI: 10.1057/9781137505781.0006

3
Legislating for Freedom

Abstract: *The first part of the chapter focuses on the legislative measures taken by the Coalition to restore civil liberties, notably under the Protection of Freedoms Act 2012. While some of the most-criticised measures taken by the New Labour governments have been repealed or limited, it is argued that these changes do little to protect civil liberties. Indeed, the latter are endangered by the as-yet unrealised promise to repeal the Human Rights Act and, most significantly, by the extensive surveillance powers of the British government and its allies (both political and corporate) which seriously threaten the right to privacy. The second part of the chapter focuses on crime prevention measures, concluding that very little has changed in practice since the New Labour years.*

Keywords: human rights; prison privatisation; Protection of Freedoms Act

Bell, Emma. *Soft Power and Freedom under the Coalition: State-Corporate Power and the Threat to Democracy.* Basingstoke: Palgrave Macmillan, 2015. DOI: 10.1057/9781137505781.0007.

For the coalition government, freedom was not only to be restored via the responsibilisation of individual citizens but also via legislation designed to reverse the New Labour trend towards increased state authoritarianism characterised by an 'abuse' and 'erosion' of 'fundamental human freedoms and historic civil liberties' (HM Government, 2010a, p. 11). Indeed, New Labour was roundly criticised across the political spectrum for having undermined basic civil liberties, notably by facilitating the collection and retention of DNA records, extending electronic surveillance and undermining basic legal protections such as trial by jury. Furthermore, although many trends predate New Labour, the governments of Tony Blair and Gordon Brown became identified with a 'new punitiveness' in the field of criminal justice (Pratt et al., 2005; Bell, 2011), as they created new offences and radically changed the sentencing laws, causing the prison population to rise exponentially to almost double the rate it had been in the early 1990s (ICPS, 2014). On taking on his role as Minister for Justice following the 2010 general election, the Conservative Kenneth Clarke described a prison population of over 85,000 individuals in England and Wales as 'quite an astonishing number' which he 'would have dismissed as an impossible and ridiculous prediction if it had been put to [him] as a forecast in 1992' (Clarke, 2010). Other prominent Conservatives attacked New Labour's record on civil liberties. David Davis, formerly shadow home secretary and once contender for the leadership of the Conservative Party, resigned his parliamentary seat in 2008 in protest at the Brown government's attempt to extend pre-charge detention for those suspected of acts of terrorism to 42 days. Davis's former Chief of Staff, Conservative MP Dominic Raab, accused New Labour of carrying out an 'unprecedented assault on our fundamental freedoms' (Raab, 2009). David Cameron largely supported these criticisms and spoke out against New Labour's legislative 'hyperactivity' which 'undermines our civil liberties' (Cameron, 2006a). Nick Clegg, as deputy prime minister, similarly declared, 'under Labour our civil liberties have been undermined, eroded, lost' and promised that 'the Coalition Government is going to turn a page on the Labour years: resurrecting the liberties that have been lost; embarking on a mission to restore our great British freedoms' (Clegg, 2011b).

The Liberal Democrats are in many ways natural advocates for freedom from excessive state interference, laying claim to a liberal tradition dating back to John Locke and John Stuart Mill. It was the Liberal Democrats who published a Freedom Bill in February 2009

DOI: 10.1057/9781137505781.0007

(Huhne, 2009), many elements of which were later taken up by the coalition government. The Conservatives too have a strong preference for freedom, stemming from the traditional conservative desire to be 'let alone' to pursue one's own interests (Aughey, 2005). Yet, there is also an authoritarian strand to conservative thought, one that has often been associated with social authoritarianism, as symbolised by section 28 (discussed earlier) but also with police authoritarianism as exemplified by the Thatcher government's conflict with the miners during the strike of 1984–5. Current Conservative Party rhetoric tends to play down such authoritarian discourse in favour of one which defends civil liberties. Downey et al. (2012, pp. 451–4) show that political opportunism played an important role here, noting how a concern with civil liberties within the Conservative Party coincided with the Conservative defeat in the 2005 general election and the subsequent need to rebrand the party, differentiating it from New Labour and from its own recent past.

This chapter will aim to determine just how deep the coalition government's commitment to restoring civil liberties really is. It will begin by examining the steps taken to protect the privacy of individuals and promote the transparency of the State. It will then look at how anti-terrorism legislation has been altered to protect basic freedoms. Finally, it will seek to determine whether the government has succeeded in reversing New Labour trends towards increasing punitiveness in the field of criminal justice. Although the government never made any express commitment to be less 'tough' in this area, it did promise to restore some basic legal protections and avoid the proliferation of new criminal offences. Less punitiveness in this field would perhaps be indicative of a more general drift away from excessive state authoritarianism.

Taming big brother?

The development of new technologies has evidently greatly increased the State's capacity to retain information about individuals. Over the past 20 years or so, a plethora of new electronic databases has been established by both private companies and government agencies to store personal data. Some of these, such as the National Identity Register and the ContactPoint Database were established under New Labour while others, although predating the New Labour governments, were vastly extended under its administration, most controversially the Police National DNA

DOI: 10.1057/9781137505781.0007

Database (NDNAD). Surveillance of individuals' movements via CCTV and of their communications via digital software was also extended. The coalition government came to power promising significant reforms to ensure that these developments would not encroach on civil liberties.

The National Identity Register, designed to retain the personal details of UK citizens issued with a biometric identity card under New Labour's identity card scheme, was destroyed in February 2011 under the *Identity Documents Act 2010* which repealed the *Identity Cards Act 2006* which had allowed for the nationwide introduction of ID cards. The ContactPoint Database, specifically designed to hold personal information about children in order to facilitate the sharing of information between agencies seeking to protect vulnerable minors, was also destroyed in August 2010. Furthermore, the *Protection of Freedoms Act 2012* outlaws routine fingerprinting of schoolchildren without parental consent. Under the same law, limits have been placed on how the NDNAD is used. In compliance with a 2008 ruling by the European Court of Human Rights (*S. and Marper v. the United Kingdom*), it is no longer possible to indefinitely retain the fingerprints and DNA profiles of anyone aged over ten arrested for a recordable offence regardless of whether or not they are actually convicted. The Coalition's programme for government promised to introduce the protections afforded to individuals under the Scottish model for DNA data retention, namely that the DNA of those who are never charged with an offence must be destroyed as soon as possible. Yet, while the 2012 law stipulates that the DNA of those people who are arrested but never convicted of an offence be destroyed, there are a number of exceptions which go much further than the Scottish model. Under the latter, those who are merely charged (but never convicted) with a serious sexual or violent offence can have their DNA retained for up to three years. Under the English model, it is not necessary to have been formally charged with such an offence – the DNA profiles of those who are arrested for 'qualifying offences' can be retained for a period of up to five years. The civil liberties organisation, *Liberty*, has expressed disappointment that the Scottish model was not adopted and also lamented the fact that those convicted of many minor offences such as begging may have their DNA profiles retained indefinitely, regardless of their age (Liberty, 2011, pp. 7–8).

Liberty has also expressed concerns that biometric ID cards have not been scrapped for foreign nationals from outside the European Union. Under European law, such individuals must carry biometric residence

DOI: 10.1057/9781137505781.0007

permits. It might be thought that it is Britain's membership of the European Union which has prompted the spread of electronic databases in the United Kingdom and that the British government is seeking to protect the freedom of British citizens from an authoritarian super state. Indeed, the European Union has developed a plethora of databases capable of storing vast amounts of personal information and carrying out surveillance across its territory (Mathiesen, 2013). For example, the Eurodac system retains biometric data from all foreign nationals who have attempted to enter the European Union illegally. The 2006 EU Data Retention Directive required service operators in member states to retain citizens' communication data (information relating to the date, time and duration – but not content – of phone and internet communications) for periods running from 6 to 24 months and to make this information available to law enforcement authorities for the purposes of crime detection. In April 2014, the European Court of Justice declared the directive invalid on the grounds of its failure to respect private life. Yet, far from welcoming this decision, the UK government rushed through emergency legislation in summer 2014, fearing that telecommunications companies would cease collecting relevant information. Under the *Data Retention and Regulatory Powers Act 2014*, UK companies may be obliged to retain communications data for a maximum period of 12 months. The law does introduce some safeguards in response to criticisms from the European Court of Justice, notably that public telecommunications operators will only be required to retain 'relevant communications data if the Secretary of State considers: that the requirement is necessary and proportionate' in the interests of national security; to protect the economic well-being of the United Kingdom 'so far as those interests are also relevant to the interests of national security'; to prevent crime or disorder, to guarantee public safety; to protect public health and/or to collect taxes owed to the UK government (section 1(1); section 3(4)). Furthermore, it includes a 'sunset clause', meaning that it is a temporary measure and is due to be repealed on 31 December 2016. Nonetheless, the new law has been widely criticised by civil liberties groups and by a minority of MPs. The UN High Commissioner for Human Rights has stated that these safeguards fall short of responding to the concerns raised by the European Court of Justice regarding the respect of the right to privacy (Travis, 2014). The government claims that the Act merely clarifies existing law by restating regulations on data retention (Clegg, 2014) and making it clear that the *Regulation of Investigatory Powers Act 2000*, concerning access to retained

DOI: 10.1057/9781137505781.0007

data and the content of communications, applies to service providers based outside the United Kingdom. However, by enshrining the extra-territorial reach of the provisions in law, the government has arguably extended its powers of surveillance outside its borders. In an open letter to the House of Commons, a group of academic experts in internet law contest the view that the legislation merely formalises the existing situation with regard to the retention of communications data and the government's right to access it. Highlighting the extra-territorial reach of the law, they conclude that it represents 'a serious expansion of the British surveillance state' (Basu et al., 2014).

The charge that Britain has become a surveillance state is given some support by revelations by Edward Snowden that GCHQ (UK Government Communications Headquarters) has had access to the NSA's (US National Security Agency) Prism programme since at least June 2010. The system was set up in 2007 to enable the United States to subvert normal legal processes to gain access to communications data stored by internet companies about foreign nationals. It was revealed that GCHQ generated 197 intelligence reports from the system in 2012 (Hopkins, 2013). The surveillance powers of the British State were already greatly extended by the *Regulation of Investigatory Powers Act 2000* which seems to have only been strengthened by the 2014 Act. While the 2000 law seeks to guarantee that surveillance powers are used in a way that is 'necessary, proportionate, and compatible with human rights', the powers conferred on the police are very wide, allowing them to demand data from telephone companies in respect of an account or an individual, and engage in covert surveillance operations themselves, intercepting communications, conducting covert surveillance and accessing encrypted electronic data.

Furthermore, CCTV surveillance systems are widespread in the United Kingdom. The British Security Industry Association estimated that there may have been as many as 5.9 million CCTV cameras in use in the United Kingdom in 2013, roughly equating with one camera for every 11 people (Reeve, 2013). Interestingly, it estimates that just one in 70 of those cameras is controlled by local government, with the rest being operated by private companies or individuals (ibid.). Such a figure may serve to undermine suggestions that the United Kingdom is a surveillance state since the State itself is not responsible for these cameras. However, the police may at any time access footage recorded by private CCTV cameras. Although the quality of such footage may

DOI: 10.1057/9781137505781.0007

be poor and many cameras are used in private rather than public areas where they would be of most value to the police, it seems that an extensive private network of CCTV cameras is capable of augmenting the existing surveillance powers of the British State. One police force, Cheshire Constabulary, has already created a register of private security cameras and encourages private operators to hand CCTV footage over to the police (Cheshire Constabulary, 2014). While public operators of CCTV cameras must now comply with a code of practice (Home Office, 2013), introduced under the *Protection of Freedoms Act 2012*, and have their activities monitored by a Surveillance Camera Commissioner, private operators face no such constraints. Police use of private CCTV footage may become a means of circumventing the new regulations.

Police surveillance powers may be further extended by the use of drones or unmanned aerial vehicles (UAVs). To date, there has been little use of drones by UK police forces. A recent survey found that 12 out of 50 police forces studied are known to have used drones for purposes ranging from the surveillance of political events to searches for missing persons (Jones, 2014). Even these forces have not used the technology regularly, partly because it is still in its infancy and subject to a number of technical problems. Yet, the study just cited notes that the United Kingdom's police forces have an 'ongoing interest' in using drones and that 'the bureaucratic and institutional infrastructure needed to advance the acquisition and use of drones by the police seems... to be firmly in place' (ibid., p. 41). Indeed, the National Police Air Service was established in October 2012 to centralise police air support services. Although these largely consist of helicopters at present, senior police figures have publicly stated that drones would be preferable to other aircraft in many cases due to their cost-effectiveness. The chief constable responsible for introducing the new service stated, 'We should be looking at different ways of providing air support in the future that don't involve putting humans up in the air, but the public need to find it acceptable and it needs to be within the law' (cited in *The Telegraph*, 2012). At the launch of the new service, the then minister for policing, Damian Green, suggested that drones 'should be treated like any other piece of police kit or activity' provided their use 'is both appropriate and proportionate' (Jones, 2014, p. 26).

Like other forms of surveillance, it will be very difficult to ensure that the use of such technology is always 'appropriate and proportionate' since once it becomes widespread it is likely to collect details about

DOI: 10.1057/9781137505781.0007

wholly innocent people. As the Snowden files revealed, the safeguards currently in place to protect citizens from the privacy abuses resulting from 'suspicionless surveillance' are at present wholly inadequate.

In theory, the *Freedom of Information Act 2000* should render government surveillance activities more transparent by enabling citizens to request access to information held by public authorities. This would imply that the United Kingdom is not a panopticon society in which the gaze of the State is only one-way – citizens are meant to be able to direct that gaze back towards the government. Indeed, a pre-election Conservative Party document, titled *Reversing the Rise of the Surveillance State*, stated, 'the government must be held accountable to the citizen, rather than the other way around' (Conservative Party, 2009, p. 9). The 2000 law (which entered into force in 2005) has often been criticised as ineffective in this respect, leading the coalition government to promise to 'extend its scope' to 'provide greater transparency' (HM Government, 2010a, p. 11). Indeed, the law sets out a large number of exceptions to the general requirement to provide information, including information relating to national security and defence, court records and the formulation of government policy to name but a few (see Part II of the Act for full details). Any information can be exempt from disclosure if it is not thought to be in 'the public interest' to release it. Under section 23 of the Act, certain public bodies including GCHQ, MI5, MI6 and the Serious Organised Crime Agency (now the National Crime Agency) are automatically exempt from the obligation to provide information to the public, regardless of whether this may be in the public interest or not. These bodies can simply answer a request for information by stating that they can neither confirm nor deny that the relevant information exists. As a result, it is impossible to know, for example, whether or not drones are owned or used by some security services in the United Kingdom (Jones, 2014, p. 30). Even where the release of information is proved to be in the public interest, this may be overridden where a minister judges that its disclosure will 'prejudice the effective conduct of public affairs' (section 36). This occurred in May 2012 when the then Minister for Health, Andrew Lansley, vetoed the release of information relating to the potential risks resulting from the Coalition's reforms of the NHS (Gay & Potton, 2014, pp. 9–11). Furthermore, private companies are wholly exempt from the legislation and even benefit from a special clause relating to commercial information held by public companies. Under section 43(2) information is exempt from disclosure if its release

DOI: 10.1057/9781137505781.0007

'would, or would be likely to, prejudice the commercial interests of any person (including the public authority holding it)'. Given the significant involvement of the private sector in the provision of public services, there is much concern that commercial exemptions from the Freedom of Information laws leave taxpayers without any means of scrutinising how their money is being spent. The Public Accounts Committee has consequently recommended that Freedom of Information be extended to public contracts with private providers (House of Commons Committee of Public Accounts, 2014) but at the time of writing the Coalition has yet to act on the recommendations, even though the Liberal Democrats have shown some support for the proposal (Rigby, 2014).

Balancing liberty and security?

The coalition government has similarly failed to significantly challenge its New Labour inheritance with regard to repressive anti-terrorism laws which undermine basic legal protections, despite the Home Secretary's declaration that the stated purpose of public protection underpinning those laws 'must never be used as a reason to ride roughshod over our civil liberties' (May, 2010a). Indeed, just two months after coming to power, the Home Secretary announced an 'urgent' review of counter-terrorism and security powers. While a number of legislative changes were introduced, anti-terrorism powers have not been fundamentally altered. Following the recommendations of the review (HM Government, 2011b, pp. 13–14), the *Protection of Freedoms Act 2012* reduced the maximum period of pre-charge detention for terrorist suspects from 28 days to 14 days (section 57). Yet, this period remains much longer than the seven-day limit in place prior to 2003. Liberty notes that it is also much longer than in most democratic countries and highlights the fact that lengthy pre-trial detention 'is more commonly associated with oppressive, non-democratic regimes' (2011, p. 21).

Existing stop and search powers under section 44 of the *Terrorism Act 2000*, which permitted the police to search anyone thought to be planning to commit an act of terrorism, even in the absence of 'reasonable suspicion', have been limited. Police must now have 'reasonable suspicion' that a person may be planning such activity before using the powers but an exception is made with regard to certain 'designated areas'. Such areas may be classified as such by a senior police officer if: he/she 'reasonably suspects that an act of terrorism will take place; and reasonably considers that the authorisation is necessary to prevent such an act; the specified area or place is no greater than is necessary to prevent such an act; and the duration of the authorisation is no longer than is necessary to prevent such an act' (section 61).

Yet, other powers to stop and search without reasonable suspicion remain in place for non-terrorist offences, notably section 60 of the *Criminal Justice and Public Order Act 1994* which enables senior police officers to authorise stops and searches for a period of 48 hours when he or she reasonably believes that serious violence may occur or that individuals may be carrying offensive weapons. Most stops and searches, however, do require reasonable grounds for suspicion under the *Police and Criminal Evidence Act 1984*, yet this does not mean that they are used in an appropriate manner, especially given the wide and varying interpretation police officers may have of the concept of 'reasonable suspicion' (Bowling & Phillips, 2007). Concerned that stop and search powers may be counterproductive in terms of police-community relations, especially when they are used in a discriminatory way, the Home Secretary Theresa May ordered an inquiry by the independent police inspectorate into how the powers are used by police forces in England and Wales (HMIC, 2013). It was found that 27 per cent of all searches did not record reasonable grounds for suspicion (ibid., pp. 29–30). In a statement to the House of Commons in April 2014, May described this as 'a worrying statistic' and announced that the *Police and Criminal Evidence Act* code of practice would be revised to ensure clarity over what exactly constitutes 'reasonable grounds for suspicion' (May, 2014a). At the time of writing, the consultation regarding this change is currently underway. It will be some time before it is clear whether these changes will significantly alter how stop and search powers are used. In terms of protecting civil liberties, such reforms are surely a step in the right direction but the legislation is still drafted rather widely, leaving senior police officers with considerable discretion over how these powers are used.

In summer 2014, at a time when the government designated the threat to Britain from terrorism as 'extreme' in response to reports that Britons who have been involved in jihadist movements in Iraq and Syria may return to the United Kingdom to launch attacks, David Cameron announced that anti-terrorism legislation would be further extended. Under the *Terrorist Prevention and Investigation Measures (TPIMs) Act 2013*,

DOI: 10.1057/9781137505781.0007

controversial 'control orders', under which the Home Secretary could decide to place foreign terrorist suspects under virtual house arrest without trial, were abolished and replaced with measures carrying the same name as the Act. TPIMs are less restrictive than control orders: they are intended to be limited to a maximum of two years (unless the Home Secretary judges the person subject to them to still represent a public danger) and they no longer force individuals to relocate far from their original place of residence. However, on 1 September 2014, the prime minister announced that this latter restriction should be re-imposed (Cameron, 2014a), despite the fact that Lord MacDonald's review of counter-terrorism and security powers declared relocation to be 'a form of internal exile, which is utterly inimical to traditional British norms' (MacDonald, 2011, p. 12). Cameron was nonetheless supported by the Independent Reviewer of Terrorism Legislation who, in a report published in March 2014, argued that while there was no need to return to the old control order system, 'locational constraints on some TPIM subjects should be stronger than has been the case' (Anderson, 2014, p. 4). While some senior Liberal Democrats, such as former leader Paddy Ashdown, criticised any further strengthening of anti-terrorism measures (Helm & Doward, 2014), Nick Clegg supported the proposals. Although he expressed some concerns about their legality, he also supported the prime minister's plans to prevent British nationals from returning to the United Kingdom if they were suspected of being involved in terrorist activity (BBC, 2014b). Such proposals would add to existing measures banning foreign nationals suspected of such activity from re-entering the United Kingdom. Should the proposed measures be accepted by Parliament, they will represent a considerable strengthening of Britain's anti-terrorism laws and a severe threat to civil liberties.

Furthermore, at the 2014 Conservative Party conference, Theresa May, the Home Secretary, promised that the 2015 manifesto would include proposals to tackle 'extremism in all its forms', in order to target activities which do not fall under the anti-terrorism laws (2014b). She announced that the government's focus should move beyond terrorism to develop a 'counter-extremism strategy' (ibid.). Proposed 'Banning Orders' and 'Extremism Disruption Orders' would curb the free speech of individuals and organisations, preventing them from expressing themselves on television or via the internet.

New powers seem unnecessary since existing anti-terrorism laws are already extremely broad and may be used to combat dangerous

DOI: 10.1057/9781137505781.0007

extremism. They already entail curtailing free speech by making the glorification of terrorism an offence (*Terrorism Act 2006*) and severely limit the freedom of those who are merely *suspected* of terrorist activity, subjecting them to highly restrictive measures without giving them the means to defend themselves in a court of law. The latest proposals to prevent British nationals from returning to the United Kingdom effectively mean condemning them to exile, even though no formal charge has been brought against them. Such measures, which undermine basic legal principles such as habeas corpus, are presented as being wholly exceptional, justified by the significant threat posed to Britain by Islamic terrorism. Yet, once enacted in law, experience shows that such measures tend to become the norm as the government effectively declares a permanent state of emergency (Joint Committee on Human Rights, 2010, pp. 7–12). Indeed, the 'exceptional' anti-terrorism measures adopted in response to the threat from Irish republican terrorism in the 1970s, such as the length of pretrial detention for terrorist suspects, extended to seven days under authorisation from the secretary of State, has now become permanently extended to 14 days under the coalition government's *Protection of Freedoms Act 2012* (and may be temporarily extended to 28 days in an emergency situation).

The normalisation of such derogations from the rule of law is often justified in the name of liberty. As the deputy prime minister stated in a joint press conference with the prime minister announcing the need for emergency legislation to access telecommunications data, 'Liberty and security must go hand in hand; we can't enjoy our freedom if we are unable to keep ourselves safe' (Clegg, 2014). In such a formulation, security is the very precondition of freedom. As such, measures which threaten to undermine the basic freedoms of some are legitimised insofar as they are seen to guarantee the security and freedom of the many and thus protect liberal values. As Cameron declared in 2014, announcing further emergency legislation:

> We are proud to be an open, free and tolerant nation, but that tolerance must never be confused with a passive acceptance of cultures living separate lives or of people behaving in ways that run completely counter to our values. Adhering to British values is not an option or a choice; it is a duty for all those who live in these islands. So we will stand up for our values; we will, in the end, defeat this extremism; and we will secure our way of life for generations to come. (2014a)

DOI: 10.1057/9781137505781.0007

Liberal democracies such as Britain declare the need to act to ensure compliance with these values. Anti-terrorism legislation which suspends certain basic liberties is said to guarantee not just the security of the nation but also its liberal values of 'openness and tolerance'. Interestingly, liberalism and security are conflated together here – they are not regarded as being fundamentally opposed, as is suggested by the oft-repeated argument that liberal democracies must find the 'right balance' between the two notions (see, e.g., Cameron, 2006a). Indeed, as Neocleous has shown, the two ideas are intimately bound up together (2007). He even argues that it is security rather than freedom that has been the ultimate goal of liberal politics since the Enlightenment due to the fact that in the absence of security the State is powerless to act in the defence of liberty (ibid., pp. 134–44). The doctrine of 'Reason of State' invoked by Locke allows the State to take whatever action is necessary to ensure its survival provided this can be justified as being in the public good (ibid., pp. 136–7). Yet while the goal of security is pursued in the name of freedom, it is in fact inimical to it: as Neocleous argues, 'the commitment to security leaves liberalism with no defence against authoritarian or absolutist encroachments on liberty, *so long as these are conducted in the name of security*' (ibid., p. 143).

Far from protecting us from the arbitrary power of the State, liberal discourse legitimises it since exceptional powers are presented as the only way to guarantee the security of the State and ultimately enable it to protect the basic freedoms and security of the people. The interests of the people and the State are conflated: the security of the latter becomes a necessary precondition for the security of the former (ibid., p. 137), just as security is regarded as a precondition for liberty.

Successive British governments have presented anti-terrorism legislation as the best means of protecting the citizenry from terrorist attacks but they fail to mention that the same laws can also be (and have been) used to protect that State from its citizens. Indeed, Parliament's Joint Committee on Human Rights expressed concern about the use of counter-terrorism powers against peaceful protesters (Joint Committee on Human Rights, 2009, pp. 26–7). Despite the Coalition's promises to 'restore rights to non-violent protest' (HM Government, 2010a, p. 11), it has in practice done little. Although section 44 of the *Terrorism Act 2000* (allowing protesters to be stopped and searched without reasonable grounds for suspicion: see above and Joint Committee on Human Rights, 2009) and section 132 of the *Organised Crime and Police Act 2005*

DOI: 10.1057/9781137505781.0007

(which prevented demonstrations from taking place in the square mile surrounding Parliament Square in London) have been repealed, protests are limited to a 24-hour period and stops and searches of protesters may still be carried out within designated areas. Much criticism was made of police handling of protests against the decision to increase university tuition fees in 2010, particularly its use of 'kettling' whereby protesters are contained in a confined area by the police and denied access to food, water or toilet facilities (Pickard, 2014). The Joint Committee on Human Rights stated that while it recognised that kettling may be necessary when protests are not peaceful, it was

> concerned about the apparent lack of opportunity for non-violent protestors to leave the contained or 'kettled' crowd, the adequacy of arrangements to ensure that the particularly vulnerable such as disabled people are identified and helped to leave the containment, and the general lack of information available to the protestors about how and where to leave. (Human Rights Joint Committee, 2011)

No government action has so far been taken to end the practice.

Such developments suggest that we ought to be wary of interpreting freedom in its most basic sense as freedom from State interference. The preceding discussion on the extended surveillance powers of the State suggest that significant State interference into our private lives is now justified on the grounds of both liberty and security. This is not to suggest that Britain is morphing into a totalitarian state whereby it is only the State that exercises surveillance over the many (what Foucault once described as the panopticon – the surveillance of the many by the few [Foucault, 1975]). The people themselves are sometimes highly supportive of measures allowing such interference into their lives, often because they believe in their capacity to make them safer. For example, the use of CCTV in public spaces is widely supported by the public: one recent survey reported that it was supported by 86 per cent of respondents (Synetics, 2014). British people are often willing participants in surveillance, handing over private information about themselves and others to both state and private agencies. They thus participate in the 'viewer society' or 'synopticon', whereby it is not just the State but society as a whole that is engaged in watching the few (Mathiesen, 1997; Davie, 2014). Far from being slaves, it seems that British people have in many ways become good liberal subjects in the Foucauldian sense of the term, internalising the need for more security and changing their behaviour appropriately to take account of new threats. Authoritarian measures are not experienced as coercion but rather as a form of 'soft' power. This is not to downplay the extensive power that the liberal state has accrued over individual citizens. Indeed, its powers of surveillance and its capacity to suspend basic legal rights apply not just to terrorists but to those who are merely suspected of such terrorist activity. *All* of us are now subjected to 'suspicionless surveillance' by the State and its private partners. This may suggest that we have moved beyond both the panopticon and the synopticon since it is no longer the few who are subjected to the view of either the minority or the majority but the many who are now subjected to the view of the many. Yet, even if surveillance has in some sense been democratised, it is the State which retains the legitimate monopoly on violence, exploiting information for its own ends.

The political philosopher Quentin Skinner is extremely critical of a liberal view of freedom which permits such extensive surveillance. He explains that 'the liberal thinks that you are free so long as you are not coerced'. Indeed, many people assume that electronic surveillance should not concern them since they personally have 'nothing to hide' and are therefore unlikely to be subject to coercion (Skinner, 2014, p. 107). This would be a limited negative conception of liberty. Skinner refutes such arguments:

> To be free we not only need to have no fear of interference but no fear that there could be interference. But that latter assurance is precisely what cannot be given if our actions are under surveillance. So long as surveillance is going on, we always could have our freedom of action limited if someone chose to limit it. The fact that they may not make that choice does not make us any less free, because we are not free from surveillance and the possible uses that can be made of it. Only when we are free from such possible invasions of our rights are we free; and this freedom can be guaranteed only where there is no surveillance. I think it very important that the mere fact of there being surveillance takes away liberty. (2014, p. 107)

Consequently, he favours what he describes as a republican conception of freedom which would guarantee freedom from the very possibility of state coercion. He does not believe that human rights alone are sufficient to protect us from such coercion. Indeed, the *Human Rights Act* in the United Kingdom, passed under the first Blair government in 1998, was incapable of protecting civil liberties from extremely coercive measures introduced by the same administration and may even have been counterproductive, lulling us into a false sense of security regarding our civil

DOI: 10.1057/9781137505781.0007

liberties (Porter, 2008). When we believe that we have certain rights, we are less likely to fight for those same rights yet, as Douzinas points out, having rights is not the same as enjoying them (2014). The right to respect for private life, for example, is one right that British citizens currently have difficulty enjoying to the full. Furthermore, the government retains a power to derogate from human rights legislation when there is a 'public emergency threatening the life of the nation' – indeed, the New Labour government did so following 9/11 in order to enable the detention of foreign terrorist suspects without trial. While the derogation was subsequently removed following a House of Lords decision in 2004 that such detention was incompatible with the *Human Rights Act*, the damage done to those who had already been imprisoned and consequently deprived from exercising their human rights was immeasurable.

Senior Conservative ministers, notably the Justice Secretary Chris Grayling, and most recently, David Cameron himself, have vowed to abolish the *Human Rights Act* (Grayling, 2013; Cameron, 2014b). It should be noted that Cameron made this pledge as early as 2006 in a speech to the right-wing think tank the Centre for Policy Studies (Cameron, 2006a). In a document laying out proposals which may be included in the Conservative Party's general election manifesto, Grayling threatened that the United Kingdom will withdraw from the European Convention on Human Rights should it not be granted a power of veto over rulings from the European Court on Human Rights (Conservative Party, 2014). Such a move would not be supported by the Liberal Democrats but the party, in common with Labour and the Conservatives, is in favour of creating a Bill of Rights. Indeed, the Coalition promised to 'establish a Commission to investigate the creation of a British Bill of Rights that incorporates and builds on all our obligations under the European Convention on Human Rights' (HM Government, 2010a, p. 11). A Commission was duly set up in March 2011 and published its final report in December 2012. Its members failed to reach agreement (Commission on a Bill of Rights, 2012) but it is unlikely that the issue has been laid to rest. The attempt to underpin rights with reciprocal duties appears to be inherently fair. Indeed, the Conservative Party has been at pains to stress that such a Bill would be a way of protecting civil liberties and human rights (Munce, 2012, p. 63). Conservatives have often suggested that ordinary people's human rights are undermined when criminals seek protection under the *Human Rights Act*. Citizens' basic liberties are said to be under threat when Human Rights legislation hinders the fight

DOI: 10.1057/9781137505781.0007

against terrorism, particularly by preventing the deportation of foreign nationals thought to pose a threat (ibid., p. 63). A Bill of Rights could therefore be presented as an inherently liberal measure while enabling the suspension of certain rights in the name of security and freedom for the majority. If such a law is enacted, it may further facilitate the accretion of state power in the name of liberty.

Reconciling freedom and justice?

The coalition government promised to take a more liberal approach to dealing with non-terrorist crimes and problem behaviour. This was to entail restoring basic legal protections such as trial by jury; refraining from creating new criminal offences; and ending a 'top-down approach' to tackling antisocial behaviour and prisoner rehabilitation, encouraging voluntary agencies and local communities to get involved. This was one more area in which the State was to be rolled back.

Certain limitations to jury trial were introduced by the *Criminal Justice Act 2003*. Section 43 allowed trials for serious or complex fraud in the absence of a jury, while section 44 allowed trials to take place without a jury where there is a 'real and present danger' of jury tampering or where jury tampering has actually taken place. Apparently following up on its promise to 'protect historic freedoms through the defence of trial by jury' (HM Government, 2010a: 11), the coalition government repealed section 43 under section 113 of the *Protection of Freedoms Act 2012*. However, section 44 remains in place. It was rumoured that the government planned to further limit the right to trial by jury after the Magistrates' Association claimed that ministers were considering reducing the number of offences that can be 'tried either way' (following the choice of the defendant) (Bowcott, 2012). In March 2014, the Lord Chief Justice appeared to question whether continuing to try fraud cases by jury was the most effective use of resources (Lord Thomas, 2014). The issue has not yet been taken up by the government, at least not in public, but it is possible that financial constraints may lead to a change of position on jury trial should a Conservative government be re-elected.

Indeed, budget constraints on the Ministry of Justice are severe with the overall budget to be reduced from almost £9 billion to £6.8 billion by the time of the general election in 2015 (Hyde, 2013). Cost considerations were already a significant factor in the government's decision to reduce

DOI: 10.1057/9781137505781.0007

access to legal aid under the *Legal Aid, Sentencing and Punishment of Offenders Act 2012*. The law ended legal aid for most clinical negligence cases, employment law cases, private family law cases, housing law cases, welfare benefits cases and immigration cases, although funding may be granted in 'exceptional' cases (notably where failure to provide legal aid would result in a breach of the European Convention on Human Rights). A report by the Judicial Executive Board, the body of senior judges advising the Lord Chancellor, measured the impact of the changes since they took effect in April 2013 (Judicial Executive Board, 2014). It found that they were often counterproductive in terms of cost, notably on account of the delays caused by the significant increase in the number of litigants in person (LiPs – those who appear in court without a legal representative). Furthermore, it stated that 'there has been a very significant impact upon the efficiency and aptitude of the courts to achieve an equitable result in those cases where LiPs are unable to afford to commission expert evidence' (Judicial Executive Board, 2014). The State has certainly 'stepped back' here but in doing so it could be said to be undermining basic freedoms regarding citizens' access to justice.

Legal protections have also been undermined after the extension of closed material procedures into civil courts under the *Justice and Security Act 2013*. Such procedures, already in use in the Special Immigration Appeals Commission (the special body that deals with appeals relating to deportation for national security reasons and appeals against the deprivation or withdrawal of British nationality or status) ensure that secret intelligence introduced by the government may only be viewed by the judge trying the case and security-cleared 'special advocates'. If it is thought to be in the public interest, those facing charges may not be informed of the evidence against them. One legal expert regrets not only the fact that the principle of open justice has been seriously undermined but also that it is now even more difficult for the public to shine a light on the workings of the intelligence services (Hickman, 2013).

With regard to the promise to 'prevent the proliferation of unnecessary new criminal offences' (HM Government, 2010a, p. 11), the State has not retreated. As promised, it did create a mechanism to try to prevent this from happening: the Criminal Offences Gateway ensures that all proposals to create new offences must first be sent to the Minister for Justice for approval. Yet, more offences are currently being created. From 1 June 2010 to 30 May 2013, 793 new offences came into force (Ministry of Justice, 2014a, p. 9). This represents a significant decrease from under

DOI: 10.1057/9781137505781.0007

the previous government when 712 new offences were created in the sole period running from 1 June 2009 to 30 May 2010 (ibid., p. 9). It should also be noted that the government continues to repeal offences: 140 were repealed in the year 2012–13 (ibid., p. 9). Yet 327 new laws were created over the same period (ibid., p. 9). As Chalmers points out, we ought to be wary of suggesting that such a legislative flurry necessarily reflects a desire for increased criminalisation on the part of the government – indeed, a significant proportion of new offences result from the need to comply with European and international obligations – but we should not assume either that much of this legislation is trivial (Chalmers, 2014, pp. 491–2): 49 per cent of the offences created in 2012–13 carried a possible custodial sentence (Ministry of Justice, 2014a, p. 7).

When it came to tackling antisocial behaviour, the coalition government was keen to mark a break with New Labour's approach which had been widely criticised as ineffective due to the high breach rate of antisocial behaviour orders (ASBOs) (Home Office, 2012). Theresa May also criticised her predecessor's 'top-down approach' to the problem, arguing that 'the people who are closest to the problem need to be driving the solution. Not civil servants in Whitehall' (2010b). To this end, the *Antisocial Behaviour Crime and Policing Act 2014* introduced a 'community trigger', meaning that local authorities and the police are now obliged to take action whenever the local community signals a particular problem to them. In this way, communities themselves are encouraged to take responsibility for the problem and to ensure that the authorities respond. While the trigger for intervention comes from the bottom-up, it is ultimately sanctions designed by the State that will be marshalled to deal with the problem.

The Home Secretary initially suggested that the new ASB sanctions should, 'where possible', 'be rehabilitating and restorative, rather than criminalising and coercive' (May 2010b). Consequently, ASB injunctions which replaced ASBOs under the 2014 law may now include positive requirements as well as prohibitions. These may take the form of attending courses or rehabilitation programmes, for example, aimed at tackling the underlying causes of antisocial behaviour. At the time of writing, the new injunctions have not yet come into force but it is likely that the adding of new requirements may simply mean that they are more likely to be breached. If they are, there is no automatic power of arrest unless it has been specified in the original injunction but a power of arrest may be sought and a prison sentence may be imposed.

DOI: 10.1057/9781137505781.0007

Previous antisocial behaviour legislation already allowed the apparatus of the State to reach further than ever before in regulating behaviour that is not covered by the criminal law. It essentially allowed the police and local authorities to intervene 'pre-crime', tackling problem behaviour before it escalated into something more serious. The new legislation may extend the reach of the State even further by subjecting antisocial behaviour to the lower civil standard of proof, allowing a court to decide whether the behaviour took place on a simple balance of probabilities. Furthermore, the definition of antisocial behaviour has been widened to include not just 'conduct that has caused, or is likely to cause, harassment, alarm or distress to any person' but also 'conduct capable of causing nuisance or annoyance to a person in relation to that person's occupation of residential premises, or conduct capable of causing housing-related nuisance or annoyance to any person' (*Antisocial Behaviour, Crime and Policing Act 2014*, Part I, section 2 (1)). It is consequently hard to see how the new measures will significantly reduce the role of the State. While communities are being encouraged to get more involved in tackling antisocial behaviour, this is only to the extent that they are to be increasingly responsibilised and encouraged to work with the agencies of government. Furthermore, communities are not to be 'liberated' from other forms of antisocial behaviour such as economic crime, environmental harm or breaches of health and safety regulation, which remain outside the reach of current antisocial behaviour legislation (Bell, 2014).

With regard to punishing offenders, the coalition government also sought to mark a break from its predecessors by focusing not just on sanctioning offenders but on ensuring that those sanctions are an effective response to crime. Consequently, it promised to introduce a 'rehabilitation revolution' which would consist in entrusting 'independent providers' with the task of reducing reoffending (HM Government, 2010a, p. 23). This focus on rehabilitation rather than punishment did indeed seem to herald a change in direction from previous policies which had led to an exponential rise in the prison population. It was a refreshing change to hear a Minister of Justice express shock at the size of the prison population and to openly doubt the effectiveness of prison in terms of rehabilitation (Clarke, 2010). Commenting on the Coalition's crime policy early into its mandate, Benyon wrote, 'the Coalition policies seem to fit more within the liberal "progressive" perspective. This tends to place more emphasis on civil liberties and rehabilitation, education

DOI: 10.1057/9781137505781.0007

and treatment for addictions and mental health problems' (Benyon, 2011, p. 150).

Just a few months after coming to power, in December 2010, the government published a Green Paper titled 'Breaking the Cycle', setting out its approach to crime reduction (HM Government, 2010b). Central to this approach was Integrated Offender Management which entailed encouraging a range of different actors – from police and probation officers to partners from the private and voluntary sectors – to work together to ensure the effective 'management' of offenders. The private sector in particular was encouraged to become more involved in the provision of employment opportunities for offenders, ensuring that 'Prisons will become places of hard work and industry' (ibid., pp. 14–17). In 2012, the Prisons Industries Unit was replaced by a government start-up, One3One Solutions, charged with getting more businesses involved in providing work for prisoners. Its website proudly boasts, 'we have 131 locations across England and Wales, utilising a workforce of motivated prisoners who are looking to repay society and build outstanding business relationships with you' (One3One Solutions, 2014). The rehabilitative value of work offered may be limited, especially if work is valued over other means of tackling offending behaviour (Bell, 2013, pp. 59–60). Yet, private companies stand to benefit significantly in terms of the relatively cheap captive labour force available to them. They also stand to benefit from probation as the majority of probation services, worth £820 million per year have been privatised (Teague, 2013, p. 17). Indeed, the Probation Service was formally dissolved in June 2014 to be replaced with 'Community Rehabilitation Companies' comprised of the private and voluntary sectors.

Even more lucrative for the private sector is its involvement in the construction and management of prisons and immigration detention facilities. The involvement of the private sector in this particular field is far from new. The first privately run prison, HMP The Wolds, opened its doors in Yorkshire in 1992. New Labour, despite its initial opposition, significantly extended the policy, contracting out a further nine prisons to the private sector. The coalition government has entered into a new, intensified prison privatisation programme. Shortly after coming to power, in July 2011, nine existing prisons in England and Wales were opened up to competition. Since the Coalition came to power, 13 publicly run prisons have been closed and a further 5 are due to close. Two new large prisons have been built (HMP Thameside and HMP Oakwood),

DOI: 10.1057/9781137505781.0007

four new mini-prisons are planned, and a 2,000-bed 'super-prison' is due to be built in north Wales, all of which will be run by the private sector.

The voluntary sector is also encouraged to get involved in the provision of offender management services. Often voluntary sector services, based as they are in the local community, are well-placed to provide specialist services. Yet, it would seem that they are increasingly crowded out of the market. As Teague has pointed out with regard to the Probation Service, a lack of funding will make it extremely difficult for the service to compete for bids on a level playing field with the private sector (Teague, 2013, p. 15). Corcoran and Hucklesby have also drawn attention to this problem and noted that third sector organisations are susceptible to mergers or even to 'being regarded as shop fronts for well-resourced private sector interests' (2013, p. 2). Furthermore, they highlight the problem of 'mission drift, whereby the values and objectives of third-sector organisations change to align more closely to government or partners agendas, to win contracts and provide services' (ibid., p. 3).

This is a trend that is likely to be exacerbated by government plans to roll out payment-by-results to all providers of services for offenders, including rehabilitative services in the community (Ministry of Justice, 2013). 'Results' are to be measured solely in terms of desistance from re-offending, measured by reconviction rates alone. This reflects a very narrow conception of rehabilitation which ignores whether or not the underlying causes of offending behaviour have actually been tackled, or whether an offender has managed to successfully (re)integrate into the community. The focus of community interventions is more likely to be on surveillance to ensure that re-offending does not occur than on supporting individuals and dealing with their problems (Clarke, 2014).

The 'rehabilitation revolution' has not resulted in a more 'liberal progressive' approach to criminal justice, contrary to what Benyon asserts (2011, p. 150). The prison population in England and Wales has continued to grow, albeit at a slower rate, under the coalition government, rising from 84,725 in 2010 (Berman & Dar, 2013, p. 4) to 85,634 at the end of September 2014 (Ministry of Justice, 2014b). This was subsequent to it having reached a peak of 88,179 prisoners on 2 December 2011 following the summer riots of the same year (Berman & Dar, 2013, p. 4). While the rhetoric of rehabilitation continues to pervade coalition policy discourse, the government has been keen to prove that it is not 'soft on crime'. The ministerial reshuffle in September 2012 which led to Kenneth Clarke being replaced by the more classically authoritarian conservative

DOI: 10.1057/9781137505781.0007

Chris Grayling as Justice Secretary would appear to be symptomatic of this concern. Tough law and order rhetoric following the 2011 riots was borne out in practice: the average custodial sentence length handed down by magistrates' courts for offences related to the riots was 5.7 months, compared to 2.5 months handed down for similar offences in the previous year in England and Wales (Berman, 2012). Furthermore, the average custodial sentence length continued to increase between 2010 and 2012 (Justice Measures, 2012). The trend towards 'preventive justice' or 'pre-crime measures' has also intensified (Ashworth & Zedner, 2014). As we noted earlier, the coalition government has not repealed measures which permit the surveillance and even detention of foreign nationals who are merely suspected of having committed a criminal offence. Similarly, measures to tackle antisocial behaviour may allow the effective criminalisation of non-criminal behaviour should conditions of injunctions be breached. In this way, the law has permitted the State to extend its reach and control over citizens' behaviour. Given its extensive powers of surveillance, we may worry about where the limits to State power lie.

Trends in the criminal justice system reflect the intensification of privatisation which may lead one to think that the State's power is more limited than before. Yet, it is the State that continues to set down the conditions under which certain functions may be contracted out and which determines how success should be measured. In the event of the private sector failing to deliver satisfactory services, it is the State that steps in to solve the problem. This occurred in 2012 when HMP The Wolds, the United Kingdom's first privately managed prison, was returned to the public sector after a number of failings were highlighted by Her Majesty's Inspectorate of Prisons (BBC, 2012). It would appear that privatisation is not driven by the desire to divest the State of key functions but rather by financial and political concerns. The Justice Secretary, Chris Grayling, in his foreword to the latest white paper on the 'rehabilitation revolution', specifically noted:

> Given the challenging financial context, we will need to increase efficiency and drive down costs to enable us to extend provision to those released from short-term sentences. We therefore intend to begin a process of competition to open up the market and bring in a more diverse mix of providers, delivering increased innovation and improved value for money. (Ministry of Justice, 2013)

Grayling expresses a hope that cost savings will be obtained by enabling 'a diverse mix of providers' to become involved in delivering criminal

DOI: 10.1057/9781137505781.0007

justice services but, as we have suggested, it is large private companies that tend to benefit from contracting out to the detriment of third sector providers. Yet, declaring an interest in involving the third sector is a politically useful way of expressing a desire to be transferring power from the State to the 'big society' and 'to portray the privatisation of prisons as a potentially progressive initiative' (Moore & Scott, 2012, p. 43). Similarly, the discourse of rehabilitation appears progressive while simultaneously allowing the government to express concern about the effectiveness of penal sanctions and appear to be tackling the crime problem. Prison labour has often, though not always, had a connotation of both rehabilitation and discipline (Harcourt, 2011, p. 237), allowing the government to straddle both punitive and progressive discourses about crime, appearing both 'liberal' and 'tough'. Yet, in practice it is state authoritarianism which remains the most salient feature of government policy. Partnership with the private sector has not weakened such authoritarianism but instead helped to mask it as the government appears to be divesting itself of key functions. Whether through building prisons or developing mass technologies of surveillance, the private sector has helped to extend the punitive apparatus of the State to the detriment of local communities and individual citizens while simultaneously improving its own profit margins.

DOI: 10.1057/9781137505781.0007

4
Economic Policy: From Small State to Big Business

Abstract: *This chapter focuses on the Coalition's economic policy, notably the two prongs of austerity and privatisation. Contrary to the TINA discourse that there is no alternative, it is shown that there was in fact an alternative to the economic policy followed. Although in reality austerity has not been as severe as originally intended, it is demonstrated that the discourse of austerity as the only possible path to follow has been effective in political terms. While government was to be deresponsibilised for tough economic decisions, citizens themselves were to be responsibilised. Yet, they have not been empowered: the main beneficiaries of economic policy have been large corporations as an ever-closer coalition of interests has been forged between the latter and the State.*

Keywords: austerity; depoliticisation; TINA

Bell, Emma. *Soft Power and Freedom under the Coalition: State-Corporate Power and the Threat to Democracy.* Basingstoke: Palgrave Macmillan, 2015. DOI: 10.1057/9781137505781.0008.

On coming to power, the Coalition sought to develop a common narrative of Britain's economic crisis. This was a narrative that was largely imposed by the Conservatives. Indeed, as noted earlier, economic policy was another 'red line' issue over which the Liberal Democrats had little negotiating power (Gamble, 2012a, p. 64). The Liberal Democrats had recognised in their 2010 general election manifesto that 'public borrowing has reached unsustainable levels' and consequently committed themselves to cutting public spending, but they argued that cuts should not be applied immediately since 'if spending [was] cut too soon, it would undermine the much-needed recovery and cost jobs' (Liberal Democrats, 2010, pp. 14–15). On forming a coalition government with the Conservatives, however, they accepted the need to make swingeing cuts immediately and consequently supported the Emergency Budget in June 2010 in which the new Chancellor, George Osborne, announced that public sector borrowing would be reduced from 10.1 per cent of GDP in 2010 to just 1.1 per cent in 2015–16 (Osborne, 2010b). Such measures were presented as necessary on account of the grave economic situation Britain was said to be in, but they also fitted nicely with the Coalition's narrative on the need to shrink the size of the State. Yet, as this chapter will seek to demonstrate, behind the rhetoric of the small State, there has actually been significant government interference in economic policy, once again undermining the Coalition's claims to be marking a significant break from the policies of their predecessors.

The politics of austerity

Both parties to the Coalition agreed on the reasons why drastic austerity measures were necessary: the economic crisis facing Britain in 2010 was not the result of a failed economic system heavily biased towards the financial sector but rather the result of the previous government's economic incompetence. This was despite the fact that Conservative economic policy between 2005, when Cameron became party leader, and 2007, with the onset of the financial crisis, had largely converged with that of New Labour, and notably favoured high spending on public services (Lee, 2011, p. 61). With the onset of the recession in 2008, the financial crisis was presented as a debt crisis, caused by Gordon Brown and the Labour Party (ibid., p. 62). The only solution was the return to a highly orthodox policy of fiscal conservatism, characterised by

DOI: 10.1057/9781137505781.0008

spending cuts and an accelerated process of privatisation. This change of tack in economic policy, supported by the Liberal Democrats in coalition government, was not driven by economic necessity. George Osborne's claim that 'the coalition Government has inherited from its predecessor the largest budget deficit of any economy in Europe with the single exception of Ireland' (Osborne, 2010b) was grossly exaggerated. Such a claim was based on absolute cash terms – given the large size of Britain's economy, it was not surprising that the deficit seemed high (Patel, 2012). Yet, when taken as a percentage of GDP, in 2010 Britain's deficit was actually lower than that of the comparable sized economies of Germany or France and was even the lowest of all G7 countries (OECD, 2014; IMF, 2010). Furthermore, it was lower than the level that Labour had inherited in 1997 and was far from being unmanageable given that Britain had the option to depreciate sterling, could rely on the Bank of England to pursue an active monetary policy and could still borrow at favourable rates on the international money markets (Gamble, 2014, p. 5). The claim that the recession was caused by government overspend-ing was also spurious given that the deficit was in fact reduced between 1997 and 2007 (OECD, 2014), even though public spending as a percent-age of GDP rose between 2001 and 2007 (*Guardian Datablog*, 2013). It only increased to levels higher than those of the previous conservative government *after* the financial crisis hit in 2008 (ibid.). It is more likely that the increase in the size of the deficit was caused by the impact of the global banking crisis from 2008 onwards (Patel, 2012).

The political nature of such a narrative was partly disguised by the creation of the Office for Budget Responsibility in 2010. The ostensibly independent panel of economic experts is charged with providing analy-sis and advice regarding the United Kingdom's economic situation. The government claims to act upon this neutral advice, thus taking some of the political heat out of economic policy decisions and giving them an air of scientific validity. In this way, austerity policy was effectively 'depo-liticised' (Byrne et al., 2012, p. 28). Yet, in practice, the State retains a highly interventionist and intrinsically *political* role in the formulation of economic policy. Indeed, for Lee (2011, p. 64) and Gamble, the Coalition's economic strategy was above all *politically* necessary: 'The opportunity to create dividing lines with Labour and to pin the responsibility for the deficit and the "decade of debt" and ever-rising borrowing on to Labour was irresistible, and George Osborne seized it with both hands' (Gamble, 2014, p. 11). The strategy was largely successful. In February 2014, a poll revealed that 33 per cent of respondents trusted David Cameron and George Osborne to run the economy responsibly, compared to 21 per cent trusting Labour leader Ed Miliband and shadow chancellor Ed Balls (*The Telegraph*, 2014). Labour, of course, is also to blame as it has not been particularly successful in challenging the Cameron/Osborne narrative, consciously deciding to focus on the future rather than going over its previous record.

George Osborne successfully presented his policy to significantly reduce public spending as 'unavoidable' and argued that 'catastrophe' would otherwise ensue (2010b). Yet, he also constantly repeated that 'fairness' underpinned policy, ensuring 'that the richest pay more than the poorest' (ibid.). This was particularly important given the widespread perception of unfairness regarding the impunity of the bankers. In an attempt to prove that the Coalition was 'a progressive alliance governing in the national interest', he vowed to support those most in need while placing the greatest burden on the broadest shoulders. Yet, austerity measures have been far from neutral. The decision to deal with the deficit via public spending reductions rather than taxation impacted most heavily on the poor and marginalised (Toynbee & Walker, 2012, pp. 47–60). A 2014 report found that the poorest 20 per cent of the population have borne 36 per cent of cuts to the social welfare budget and to local government (Duffy, 2014, p. 13). Similarly, a 2013 report by the New Economics Foundation found that it is the unemployed, low-income earners, the very elderly, the young and the disabled who are disproportionately affected by austerity measures, notably the limitation of social care, child care, youth services, housing services, and legal advice (Slay & Penny, 2013). The decision to increase VAT to 20 per cent also bears down disproportionately on those who are least well-off, given that they spend a higher percentage of their income on taxable goods.

Meanwhile, the top rate of income rate was cut from 50 per cent to 45 per cent and David Cameron has refused to rule out a possible cut to 40 per cent should the Conservatives win the 2015 general election (Parker, 2014). Indeed, it is likely that a future Conservative government would reduce taxes for the highest earners by increasing the income threshold above which people will have to pay the 40 per cent rate. Companies have also benefitted from tax changes. Corporation tax was slashed from 28 per cent to just 21 per cent and is due to fall to 20 per cent by 2015, which will make it the lowest rate in the G20 (HM Government, 2013). Jenkins describes this as a 'reckless' measure from a purportedly 'austere' chancellor (Jenkins, 2014). Further tax breaks for companies also seemed to undermine the discourse of austerity. Under the new Controlled Foreign Company Regime, profits earned by overseas subsidiaries of British companies are exempt from UK taxation, while the 'Patent Box system' enables companies to apply a rate of just 10 per cent corporation tax to profits earned from its patented inventions.

Such policies suggest that austerity policies have in practice been highly selective, leading Jenkins to affirm that 'Osborne has been no iron chancellor. He is firmly in the mould of Gordon Brown and Alistair Darling – high spending, high borrowing and a sucker for every trendy aircraft carrier, railway or wind turbine going' (Jenkins, 2014). He argues that he has been an astute politician, showing 'stern austerity towards the outside world and a wholly different approach towards the public finances' (ibid.). Indeed, while public sector expenditure has decreased from 42.2 per cent as a percentage of GDP in 2009–10 to 40.8 per cent in 2013–14, it remains higher than it was in 2008–9 (39.4 per cent) (HM Treasury, 2014, p. 61). It is the rhetoric of austerity that has been more important than reality and helped the Conservative Party to claw back its reputation for economic competence from Labour. It is also such rhetoric that has been ideologically important for the party, enabling it to appear to be shrinking the State. It was no coincidence that some of the most severe spending cuts affected local authorities (HM Treasury, 2014, pp. 20–34), forcing them to seek funding from the private and voluntary sectors and thus engage with the government's 'Big Society' project.

Corporate welfare

The coalition government has in practice remained highly interventionist in economic policy. Although it may have attempted to wean some parts of society off the State by cutting benefits, we saw in Chapter 2 the extremely interventionist, authoritarian policies that have been adopted in an attempt to change perceived cultural attitudes towards welfare. Furthermore, while welfare has been limited for those at the bottom of the social ladder, corporate welfare has been extended, arguably expanding rather than shrinking the role of the State. It might even be asserted that there is a veritable 'culture of *corporate* dependence on state support' (Shutt, 2012, *my italics*). Corporate welfare is defined as 'public policies that directly or indirectly meet the specific needs and/or preferences

DOI: 10.1057/9781137505781.0008

of private businesses' (Farnsworth, 2013, p. 51). Indeed, apart from benefitting from favourable fiscal regimes, as noted earlier, the sector also benefits from important state subsidies. This is particularly true of the financial sector. In order to save major banks such as Northern Rock from collapse, state subsidies were awarded, amounting to £512 billion for the British taxpayer (NAO, 2010). For the New Economics Foundation, while this 'bail-out of the private sector by the public purse' was on an 'unprecedented scale', it represents only one part of the state support for banks and the financial services sector since they also benefit from a whole range of hidden subsidies (Prieg & Greenham, 2011, p. 2). For example, the 'quantitative easing windfall subsidy' effectively allows banks to make a substantial amount of money through trading in gilts and corporate bonds (ibid., pp. 7–8). This practice became considerably more profitable following the Bank of England's adoption of a policy of quantitative easing in 2009 via which it increased the amount of money available in the economy by buying government bonds, often from high street banks. Despite the fact that the policy places a significant amount of power in the hands of central bankers, furthering the trends towards the depoliticisation of economic policy (Sowells, 2014, p. 175), it is sanctioned by the Treasury, effectively allowing government to artificially control the amount of money circulating in the economy. While some economists have a rather favourable view of the effects of the policy in terms of boosting overall GDP, others argue that it has mainly benefitted the financial services sector (ibid., pp. 178–9).

The private sector more generally has benefitted from the accelerated pace of privatisation, actively encouraged by the coalition government as part of its 'Big Society' agenda. While the government did not explicitly promote privatisation as a key policy, the Conservative manifesto had promised to 'increase the private sector's share of the economy in all regions of the country' (Conservative Party, 2010). This promise seems to have been fulfilled, although not so much via direct sell-offs of public assets, as was common during the Thatcher years, but rather via the localism agenda. As discussed in Chapter 1, it is the private sector to the detriment of the third sector and local communities that has benefitted from policies which ostensibly reduce the role of the State in the delivery of local services. As an example, a report for the House of Commons Public Administration Committee noted that 16 out of 18 contractors for services in the Work Programme are actually private sector companies (2011, p. 40). A more recent House of Commons report lamented the

DOI: 10.1057/9781137505781.0008

fact that 'so far, the contracting out of services has led to the evolution of privately owned public monopolies, who largely, or in some cases wholly, rely on taxpayers' money for their income' (House of Commons Committee of Public Accounts, 2014, p. 3). There is indeed a limited variety of private sector service providers in the United Kingdom. For instance, the 14 privately run prisons in England are managed by just three companies: G4S Justice Services, Serco Custodial Services and Sodexo Justice Services. These companies are involved in several sectors, providing healthcare and welfare-to-work services, for example. The Coalition's healthcare reforms under the *Health and Social Care Act 2012*, which force GPs to form private consortia together with other healthcare professionals, are also likely to benefit these companies since the consortia will be encouraged to buy patient services on the open market. Private companies providing public services are already heavily subsidised by the UK government: a 2013 report from the National Audit Office estimated that contracting out to the private sector represents approximately half of the £187 billion that the public sector spends on goods and services each year (NAO, 2013a, pp. 6–10). Even more straightforward privatisations, notably the sale of Royal Mail, in autumn 2013, are heavily subsidised by the government (and ultimately the taxpayer). It is estimated that Royal Mail was undervalued at the time of its sale by approximately £1 billion (Business, Innovation and Skills Committee, 2014).

The private sector has also benefitted directly from austerity policies. As Macartney points out, the government has encouraged the increase of consumer debt by reducing state benefits to such low levels (2011). Whether this was deliberate or not, increasingly people are obliged to turn to extraordinarily high interest rate loans, notably so-called 'payday loans' to fund everyday living costs. Unsurprisingly, the Provident Financial Group, the United Kingdom's largest personal loan company, was extremely positive about the government's comprehensive spending review which promised to slash benefit levels.

Light-touch regulation

Given the extensive benefits conferred on private companies by the government, it is to be expected that the former are subject to a number of stringent conditions. Indeed, contracts for the provision of services are often highly detailed and failure to meet the requirements therein

DOI: 10.1057/9781137505781.0008

may lead to the contract being revoked. Yet, the House of Commons Committee of Public Accounts found that often there is insufficient oversight of these contracts. The Committee outlined a number of problems in this respect: the government's failure to require that open-book accounting methods are used by private companies; its failure to adequately oversee the day-to-day operation and delivery of services; its failure to impose sufficiently deterrent penalties for contract failure; its lack of adequate contract management skills; and the inadequacy of whistle-blowing mechanisms when things go wrong (House of Commons Committee of Public Accounts, 2014). It remains to be seen whether improvements will be made to ensure that companies provide quality services to the public. So far, the government's approach has not been particularly stringent. Despite the discovery that G4S and Serco had been overcharging the Ministry of Justice for electronic monitoring services for a period of eight years (NAO, 2013b), leading to an ongoing investigation by the Serious Fraud Office, the company has continued to be awarded new contracts.

The coalition government also adopted an extremely lenient approach to financial services regulation despite having declared that 'the current system of financial regulation is fundamentally flawed' (HM Government, 2010, p. 9). A veritable litany of misconduct has marred the sector over the past few years: over-investment in the sub-prime market, leading to the near collapse of British banks Northern Rock, the Royal Bank of Scotland (RBS) and HBOS; mis-selling of ineffective additional insurance policies, prompting the Payment Protection Insurance (PPI) scandal; the fixing of the London inter-bank lending rate (LIBOR) and the foreign exchange market (FOREX) rate, causing savers and investors to lose huge amounts of money; money-laundering operations in countries such as Libya, Myanmar, Sudan and Iran. In response, the coalition government claims to have 'introduced the biggest reforms to the banking sector in a generation' (HM Government 2014) via the *Financial Services Act 2012* and the *Financial Services (Banking Reform) Act 2013*. Under the first of these laws, the government made the manipulation of LIBOR a criminal offence. It also set up a new regulatory structure for the banking and financial services industry by abolishing the Financial Services Authority in April 2013 and replacing it with two new authorities, the Financial Conduct Authority (FCA), charged with regulating the financial services industry, and the Prudential Regulation Authority (PRA), charged with regulating banks, building societies, credit unions, insurers and major

DOI: 10.1057/9781137505781.0008

investment firms. In 2014, a new LIBOR administrator took over from the British Bankers Association: NYSE Euronext, parent company of the New York Stock Exchange, has been fixing LIBOR rates under the regulation of the FCA as of February 2014. The *Banking Reform Act* seeks to introduce greater accountability in banking by introducing a new Senior Persons Regime which will make senior managers and directors liable for misconduct unless they can prove that they took all reasonable steps to prevent it from occurring or continuing. Where such persons are found to be guilty of reckless misconduct, they may now face a prison sentence of up to seven years and/or a fine (section 36). Furthermore, a 'ring-fence' has been placed around the deposits of individuals and small businesses in an effort to separate retail and investment banking activities, but the government steered clear of full structural separation.

These reforms are unlikely to bring about fundamental change. It has been suggested that the reforms made to the LIBOR rate-setting process are unlikely to tackle the fundamental problem with the benchmark process, namely that it is based on entirely virtual rates rather than on real market value (*Financial Times*, 2012), leaving it open to the risk of manipulation. Furthermore, the new LIBOR administrator, NYSE Euronext, is far from independent given its concurrent role as a commodities exchange. The creation of a new regulatory regime will not necessarily bring about fundamental change either. First, regulators must be provided with adequate financial resources: the director of the Serious Fraud Office claimed that budgetary constraints had been a key factor in his decision not to pursue a criminal investigation into the LIBOR scandal when he first became aware of it in summer 2011 (Binham, 2012). Secondly, given the complex structure of banking today, it is very hard for regulators to trace lines of accountability and to determine what is really going on at the top – as one peer pointed out in a debate on the Banking Reform Bill, it may be that banks are not just too big to fail but also simply too big to regulate (Lord McFall of Alcluith, 2013). Finally, as the Parliamentary Committee on Banking Standards report noted, changes in the law will not suffice to bring about reform without a change of approach on the part of the regulators who have often contented themselves with mere box-ticking rather than in-depth investigation (Parliamentary Commission on Banking Standards, 2013, pp. 140–4).

Senior legal experts have also suggested that it is unlikely that the criminal sanctions which may be brought under the new 'Approved

DOI: 10.1057/9781137505781.0008

Persons Regime' will lead to successful prosecution of those responsible for serious misconduct in banking. Indeed, it may be difficult to prove the direct responsibility of those responsible for banking failures given the definitional problems that may arise from determining whether or not an employee could indeed be classified as a 'senior manager', or as someone authorised to carry out a 'senior management function' (Coltart, 2014). Furthermore, causation may be hard to prove between the act of recklessness and its consequences (ibid.), especially given the scale of current banking operations, many of which take place outside national borders. One senior lawyer concluded that the law therefore 'smacks of sabre-rattling and political point-scoring' (ibid.).

Finally, the proposals on ring-fencing have been subject to serious criticism given that the system currently lacks sufficient 'electrification' to ensure that the boundary between retail and investment banking activities is respected. Indeed, the Parliamentary Commission on Banking Standards had insisted on the need for electrification to at least threaten banks with full separation if the fence is not respected (Parliamentary Commission on Banking Standards, 2013, p. 170). The *Banking Reform Act* proposed that before taking a bank before a tribunal to enforce the ring-fence, the regulator must first serve three preliminary notices and seek permission from the Treasury on each occasion (section 4). A peer commented on the Bill: 'What we have now is not a ring-fence; I suggest that it is a hammock in which the executives can swing easily above the ground, while all the hassle takes place on the ground with the politicians and the regulators, and the executives look down from above, easy and relaxed' (Lord McFall of Alcluith, 2013).

The relatively lenient treatment of companies who fail to meet their duties to the public can be starkly contrasted with the government's approach to ordinary citizens who are thought to flout their duties to find work and support themselves and their families. This reflects the fact that companies are increasingly accorded special citizenship status (see Bell, *forthcoming*, 2016). While the notion of corporate citizenship is often thought to be synonymous with that of 'corporate responsibility' according to which corporations owe key duties to civil society, it has in reality come to signify that corporations, like ordinary citizens, may also exercise certain rights vis-à-vis the State. These include the traditional rights of citizenship, namely civil, political and social rights. Indeed, corporations exercise civil rights as legal entities, entitled to the protection of the law; they exercise political rights, participating in the political process as members of powerful lobby groups and as partners in governance; they exercise social rights as the beneficiaries of multifarious forms of state welfare. Yet, in practice companies are accorded a privileged citizenship status since, contrary to the Coalition's pledge to enable all citizens to become involved in governance, it is corporations who have become privileged partners and face limited sanctions when they fail to live up to their duties as 'citizens'.

A solid coalition of interests

While the power of corporations was significantly increased under the Coalition, facilitated by corporate welfare and light-touch regulation, this does not mean that the power of the State was correspondingly weakened. The State played a significant role in engineering the increase of corporate power and itself benefitted in political terms from this development. State power and corporate power are in reality mutually reinforcing as the two sectors have come to share a coalition of interests. It could be argued that it is this coalition which is more powerful than the political coalition which exists between the Liberal Democrats and the Conservatives.

The strength of this coalition may appear to lie in the degree of influence that corporate power has over government. Such influence is of course extremely difficult to measure but lobbying activity and financial donations are often taken as an indicator. Donations from the financial sector to the Conservative Party during the last election year are reported to have accounted for more than half of all party funding that year (Mathiason & Bessaoud, 2011). It is of course difficult to prove the link between such funding and the adoption of particular policy initiatives, yet significant funding can ensure that certain individuals have direct access to government ministers. Indeed, individuals making donations of over £50,000 each are entitled to membership of the 'Leader's Group', a privileged circle of people who are given opportunities to meet the prime minister at Conservative Party events. Often such donations are not even necessary to gain access to such privileged circles. The 'revolving door' that exists between the private and public sectors show that the boundaries between them are extremely permeable (Millar & Dinan, 2009). Indeed, current senior ministers David Laws and Oliver Letwin both worked in investment banking (Cave, 2013b) while former Labour

DOI: 10.1057/9781137505781.0008

ministers Lord Peter Mandelson and Jacqui Smith left government to become advisers to Ernst & Young and Deloitte respectively (Sikka, 2011).

Financial donations and lobbying are likely to be closely linked, suggesting that those with the most money have the loudest voice in the lobbying process. In the run-up to the last general election, David Cameron himself expressed concern about people 'buying power and influence' and promised to '[shed] the light of transparency on lobbying in our country' (Cameron, 2010e). Consequently, the *Transparency of Lobbying, Non-party Campaigning and Trade Union Administration Act* was passed in 2014. Consultant lobbyists must now have their details entered on a new register of consultant lobbyists if they wish 'to carry on the business of consultant lobbying' (section 1(1)). This means that they must register their name, their client information and the name of the person or persons on whose behalf the lobbying is to be done if it is being done for payment (section 4). But there is no obligation to provide information regarding the purpose of the lobbying. Furthermore, by restricting its remit to 'consultant lobbyists', the Act excludes four out of five paid lobbyists, namely all in-house lobbyists, business lobby groups, charities and trade unions (Cave, 2013a). Such a limited piece of legislation is extremely unlikely to change deeply ingrained practices, especially given the fact that lobbying is now an integral part of the process of government (Cave and Rowell, 2014). Indeed, ministers have to a great extent come to rely on lobbyists as a source of information and they find it increasingly difficult to resist the pressures of the most powerful among them. The United Kingdom is particularly vulnerable to the pressures of lobbyists working on behalf of large multinational corporations owing to its 'disproportionate dependency on mobile capital' which has left it open to blackmail by companies threatening to leave the country, taking their investment elsewhere (Farnsworth, 2006, p. 85).

Representatives from large corporations are welcomed into the heart of Westminster to provide consultancy services. For example, the world's four biggest accountancy firms, KPMG, PWC, Ernst & Young and Deloitte, advise government on tax law and contracting out (Cave, 2013b). It would surely be naïve to suppose that this does not give them a certain degree of influence over the policy-making process. It would also be naïve to assume that central government can possibly be solely responsible for decision-making as the structure of government has become increasingly complex. Indeed, the UK government today goes

DOI: 10.1057/9781137505781.0008

far beyond the departments of state. There are also non-ministerial departments, public corporations, executive agencies, national special health authorities, advisory non-departmental public bodies, tribunal non-departmental public bodies, executive non-departmental public bodies and independent monitoring boards (Flinders, 2006, p. 227). Consequently, 'the role of central departments has changed from administering public policy to co-ordinating the web of organizations, each of which enjoy different degrees of autonomy, to which implementation has now been delegated' (ibid., p. 227). Central government simply no longer has the capacity to develop policy alone. Nor does it necessarily believe that it has the expertise, given the decline of faith in the expertise of government bureaucrats from the 1970s onwards (Bevir, 2010, p. 27). Subcontracting means than the State gradually loses competence with regard to certain activities it used to perform, meaning that it increasingly has to rely on outside contractors to tell it how to act: 'Government becomes a kind of institutional idiot' (Crouch, 2012, p. 41). This is likely to have left it particularly open to influence from third parties, particularly large corporations that claim to have the required level of expertise to understand the complexities of policymaking.

Consequently, the power of corporations goes beyond the mere influence that may be exercised by lobbyists. As governments increasingly contract out public service delivery to the private sector, the latter comes to assume some of the key functions of government, notably determining access to certain services. For example, ATOS, the international IT services company, under government contract to carry out 'work capability assessments' can determine whether or not welfare claimants should continue to receive benefits or whether they are 'fit for work'. Crouch suggests that firms have actually become policymakers themselves as governments have withdrawn from public service provision (2010, p. 166). He gives the example of company-led pension policy which, as we noted earlier, is moving increasingly towards the private sector. It would therefore be a mistake, he argues, to consider large corporations as little more than a powerful lobby since they have now become 'part of the polity, insiders, not a part of an external civil society that powerfully lobbies the polity' (ibid., p. 167). Such a view is shared by Wilks who believes that the business corporation has become 'a governing institution which has transcended mere political influence to become a vehicle of government with a partnership status in making and implementing public policy' (2013, p. 62).

DOI: 10.1057/9781137505781.0008

None of this may seem particularly new. Under past periods of liberal government, powerful capitalists were actively involved in government policymaking as members of Parliament. In 1865, for example, almost one quarter of MPs were railways directors who sought to gain handsomely from unregulated market in the field – this may have had some influence on their reluctance to legislate to regulate the activities of speculators in the nascent industry (Robb, 2002, p. 43). Yet, there are some key differences in the era of neoliberal government. Most significantly, as Anthony Sampson points out, the new class of wealthy people who have made their fortunes in the City or through working for multinational companies have quite different attitudes to their predecessors: they have no sense of social obligation to their own locality or country as they are now able to move just as freely as their capital, crossing international boundaries and setting up home or business where they wish (Sampson, 2005, pp. 339–48). Despite all the talk about corporate responsibility, contemporary corporations and individuals can divest themselves of these obligations at the drop of a hat. Corporate citizens are now global citizens: they owe no special duties to their nation-states, despite the privileges conferred upon them by those same states.

Given that they are now part of the polity, this has serious consequences for democracy. Unlike elected representatives, they are not accountable to the people: 'giant corporations constitute a non-democratic part of the modern polity' (Crouch, 2010, p. 168). This is particularly problematic, given that they have taken over may state functions, notably with regard to public service delivery. Individual citizens have no direct way of holding them to account: they can only be held to account by the government. Yet, we have seen that government does a poor job of overseeing the contracts of its service providers. This does not mean that it is weak, however. It is simply not the case that 'the centre of gravity of the power-world [has been] shifting away from Westminster towards the City' (Sampson, 2005, pp. 360–1). The real loss of power has been that of ordinary citizens. While it is clear that citizen power has always been limited, at least in the more recent past government's primary role was to protect the citizenry by guaranteeing minimum social and economic security and providing public services. Today, its main efforts are directed at enhancing the opportunities of the private sector for capital accumulation by 'liberating' these services from public control and 'freeing' the people from the State by granting them greater market choice in services. In doing so, it assumes an extremely interventionist role in

DOI: 10.1057/9781137505781.0008

economic policy, putting in place favourable fiscal regimes and setting up the regulatory structures necessary to oversee the process of market liberalisation. Yet, it is also obliged to assume an extremely interventionist role vis-à-vis the people who are to be persuaded that these reforms are in their best interests.

Constructing a new common sense

Many people in Britain do not seem entirely convinced that the key prongs of coalition economic policy are working in their best interests. Despite a recent poll showing that the Conservatives are the party most trusted to handle the economy responsibly, most voters do not believe that their policies can improve their day-to-day financial situation, notably by tackling the high costs of living (*The Telegraph*, 2014). People generally oppose privatisation: 36 per cent of people polled in summer 2013 declared that they were 'strongly opposed' to the privatisation of Royal Mail, with a further 31 per cent stating that they 'tend[ed] to oppose' the sell-off (YouGov, 2013). Just 4 per cent of those polled stated that they 'strongly supported' it (ibid.). There is also opposition to the increasing involvement of the private sector in the NHS (IPSOS/MORI, 2013). Furthermore, the majority of voters do not seem to have accepted the dominant narrative presented by the coalition government that the previous Labour government was responsible for the UK financial crash in 2008: a poll carried out in May 2014 showed that over 53 per cent blame the banking industry (Survation/Progressive Polling, 2014). Nonetheless, there seems to be a grudging acceptance of the status quo, despite some popular mobilisation in the form of the Occupy movement or the UK Uncut campaign. This is what Gilbert describes as 'disaffected consent wherein a general dissatisfaction with neoliberalism and its social consequences is very widespread, but no popular alternative is able to crystallise or cohere with sufficient potency to develop the necessary critical mass to challenge neoliberal hegemony' (Gilbert, 2013a, pp. 18–19).

A neoliberal 'hegemony', while never complete (Hall, 2012, p. 25), has indeed been in the process of creation over the past 30 years and more. Political elites have sought to construct a particular narrative which legitimises neoliberal policies of welfare state retrenchment and market deregulation. In the process of constructing such a hegemony,

DOI: 10.1057/9781137505781.0008

the current crisis of neoliberal capitalism has been reconstructed not as a financial crisis but as a debt crisis provoked by the policies of the previous Labour government. The government has been greatly aided in this endeavour by the mainstream media. Reconstruction of the narrative of crisis was important since it enabled the coalition government to mark a break with previous policy while pursuing what may be understood as an essentially 'restorationist' project, which has entailed reverting to 'business as usual' and pursuing essentially the same neoliberal policies as in the past (namely increased marketisation) (Seymour, 2010, pp. 16–17; Clarke, 2012, pp. 49–50). The discourse of crisis justified the adoption, not of policies that would announce a radical change of direction and tackle the causes of the crash at source, but rather of a radical policy of austerity that would leave the neoliberal system intact. Following Thatcher, this was in turn justified by the discourse of TINA ('there is no alternative'). Cameron declared, 'If there was any other way I would take it. But there is no alternative' (Cameron, 2013b).

Yet, there was also a discourse of modernity that sought to present the Conservative approach as somewhat different from the past. Osborne promised to adopt 'a new model of economic growth', accompanied by new institutions such as the Office for Budget Responsibility. Allowing independent rather than government experts to advise on economic policy fitted neatly with the Coalition's broader modernist discourse on the limitation of state power. While modernity and progress were once concepts associated predominantly with the Labour Party or, at times, the Liberal Party, the Conservatives have usually been associated with the defence of tradition. But for Cameron, as for Thatcher before him, it was important to appropriate this language in order to present the post-war social democratic consensus as a thing of the past and a return to economic liberalism as the future (Seymour, 2010, p. 65). Such language conveniently masks the restorationist nature of the project.

Apportioning the blame to its political predecessors also allowed the Coalition to 'nationalise' what was in reality a global crisis, thus justifying swift and drastic action on the part of the nation-state (Clarke, 2012, p. 50). Importantly, it enabled the government to 'personalise' the crisis, associating it not with faceless international capitalism but rather with individual citizens in Britain. The real problem was one of *irresponsibility*: the irresponsibility of the previous government but also the irresponsibility of individuals that has resulted from the excessive growth of the State (Clarke & Newman, 2014). Through their dependence on the State,

DOI: 10.1057/9781137505781.0008

benefit claimants had indirectly caused the crisis by encouraging the State to overspend to meet their needs. The crisis was thus also transformed into a crisis of morality. While the government did make some noises about the questionable morality of bankers, its main focus has been on the morality of individuals. The moral notion of 'fairness' has been linked not with the 'unfairness' of the power and wealth of the elites compared to the modest means of the masses but rather to the 'unfairness' of benefit recipients receiving more than those who 'work hard' (ibid., p. 312). The discourse of 'we are all in this together' justifies the promotion of individual responsibility and sacrifice. While the discourse may be new, the result is the same as under previous governments from Thatcher through to Blair: those who are not seen to be 'pulling their weight' are easy targets for demonisation.

Here too, the State has played a significant role, adopting a wide variety of policies designed to encourage individual responsibility, from the localism agenda discussed in Chapter 1 to the limitation of state support analysed in Chapter 2. The narrative of responsibility has been enforced by authoritarian means, further reinforcing the argument that state power has not been relinquished. As this chapter has sought to demonstrate, even while divesting itself of social responsibilities by outsourcing public services and limiting the welfare state, the State has been highly active. It may have helped to boost the power of the private sector by promoting 'aggressive privatisation' (Seymour, 2010, p. 3) against the public will and allowing the financial sector to recover via its policy of quantitative easing but there has in no way been a trade-off for its own power. If anything, state power has probably been reinforced as the government takes the credit for Britain's slow (but fragile) economic recovery.

DOI: 10.1057/9781137505781.0008

5
Exporting Soft Power

Abstract: *The focus of this chapter is on foreign policy. The 'liberal' conservative approach of the coalition government is characterised by a 'soft' rather than 'hard' approach, seeking to spread influence abroad via international aid and cultural programmes rather than through military intervention. This liberal approach masks authoritarianism since, rather than furthering the interests of local peoples, humanitarian intervention is primarily used to further British interests, enabling the state to project a positive image abroad and British corporations to benefit from new contracts providing consulting services to developing states and investing in newly privatised industries and services.*

Keywords: Europe; foreign policy; liberal interventionism; soft power

Bell, Emma. *Soft Power and Freedom under the Coalition: State-Corporate Power and the Threat to Democracy.* Basingstoke: Palgrave Macmillan, 2015. DOI: 10.1057/9781137505781.0009.

While the discourse of 'freedom, fairness and responsibility' was most readily identified with domestic policy under the coalition government, these values were also to inform foreign policy (HM Government, 2010, p. 20). As in other policy areas, it was important for the Conservatives to mark a break with the policies of both the former Labour and Conservative governments, as part of their modernisation project. They thus attempted to combine the classical conservative 'realist approach' to foreign policy with a new emphasis on its humanitarian/ethical dimension, as promoted by Robin Cook as Foreign Secretary under the first Blair government from 1997 to 2001. The 'realist' part of this approach entailed being sceptical about the possibility of implementing any kind of grand plan or following any distinct ideology; the acceptance that appeasement cannot work; and recognising the need to work within the confines of international structures which can confer legitimacy on foreign intervention (Daddow, 2013, p. 116). As for the humanitarian aspect, this was enshrined in the commitment to spread the values of freedom and democracy and to uphold human rights across the globe. This dual approach was summed up as 'liberal conservatism', a concept most famously outlined in Cameron's 2006 speech as leader of the Opposition (Cameron, 2006b). It meant realistically assessing the threats to Britain from abroad, accepting 'that democracy cannot quickly be imposed from outside', understanding that military action alone will not suffice, and recognising that foreign policy must be informed by multilateralism. But, perhaps more idealistically, it meant acting 'with moral authority' (ibid.). Although outlined by the Conservative leader, the policy also sat well with Liberal Democrat policy, summed up in their 2010 manifesto as putting 'British values of decency and the rule of law back at the heart of our foreign policy' (Liberal Democrats, 2010).

In government, this has been one policy area 'where unity between the Conservatives and the Liberal Democrats has been almost flawless' (Auda-André, 2014, p. 246). Indeed, there was broad consensus within the government about the need to intervene in Libya in 2011 in order to stop the Qadhafi regime's attacks on civilians which the UN Security Council had judged 'might constitute crimes against humanity' (UN Resolution 1973). Most recently, there was approval across the Coalition for the decision taken in September 2014 to carry out air strikes against Islamic State of Iraq and the Levant (ISIL) in Iraq.

DOI: 10.1057/9781137505781.0009

Recent policy in Iraq seems to represent the perfect example of 'liberal conservatism' as a 'realistic' strategy informed by both self-interest and humanitarian concerns:

> We have a comprehensive strategy for action. As I have said, we have a clear request from the Iraqi Government. We have a clear basis in international law. We have a substantial international coalition, including many Arab partners, and we need to act in our own national interest. So I believe that it is morally right that we now move to a new phase of action by asking our armed forces to take part in international air strikes against ISIL in Iraq, and I believe we should do so now. (Cameron, 2014c)

The government claims to be restoring freedom not just to its own citizens, by protecting them from a security threat, but also to foreign peoples at risk from dictatorial regimes or extremist groups. It is the liberal discourse of rights that underpins policy but realism is never far away. Indeed, despite Conservative criticism of human rights at home, Cameron's foreign policy, at least under William Hague as Foreign Secretary from 2010 to summer 2014, appeared to have 'a strong commitment to human rights at its core' (Beech & Munce, 2014). Beech notes that the Coalition's humanitarianism in foreign policy has much in common with New Labour's 'liberal interventionism' yet he argues that it is nonetheless imbued with a more traditional conservative approach to foreign policy which entails defending Britain's national interests and adopting a much more cautious approach to the use of hard power to achieve these ends (Beech, 2011a). For Daddow and Schnapper, conservative realism certainly continues to inform foreign policy: the liberal approach is 'bounded' by pragmatism which prevents policy from becoming overly ideological (2013). Honeyman, however, suggests that it was a more muscular liberalism that won out over conservative realism, arguing that 'Liberal Conservatism' was 'short-lived' once the Coalition was actually in power, tested to its limits by the military intervention in Libya which notably entailed pushing for democracy by force (2012, p. 134). Yet, the need to deploy the 'muscle' of the state can also be regarded as being informed by Conservative realism, provided such action is approved by international structures.

As with domestic policy, a certain assertion of state power is justified in the name of liberty. From time to time, as in Iraq, 'hard power' will need to be invoked whereby the state assumes its classic regalian functions. But a liberal policy also requires the deployment of 'soft power' which may enable the British government to extend its influence and spread humanitarian values throughout the world. Yet, it has been asserted that in exercising soft power, Britain is in reality adopting a policy of 'liberal imperialism' whereby humanitarian interests come secondary to national imperial interests which continue to be pursued by more subtle means than in the past (Rustin & Massey, 2014).

Soft power and corporate imperialism

While the Coalition agreed that it was necessary to deploy 'hard power' with regard to Libya and Iraq, this was only pursued as a last resort. The emphasis of contemporary British foreign policy is on 'soft power'. As William Hague declared as foreign secretary, 'Our history is often one of hard power. But in the coming years we will do even more to unleash these rivers of soft power across the world, so that we cultivate influence that flows rather than power that jars' (Hague, 2014). 'Soft power' may be preferred for sound pragmatic reasons, not least of which is the current state of British public finances which led to significant cuts in the defence budget (Chalmers, 2013). Yet, it may also be pursued for political reasons: in particular, a focus on humanitarian aid and international development can give a more ethical dimension to foreign policy, thus legitimising intervention.

While many tools may be used to spread soft power, international aid in particular stood out as a key policy under the Coalition, fitting nicely with broader 'liberal conservative' policy. There was cross-party commitment to increasing the amount of foreign aid to 0.7 per cent of national income in line with UN targets (Honeyman, 2011, p. 129), a target surpassed by the United Kingdom in 2013 (Booth, 2014, p. 8). David Cameron himself is reportedly passionately committed to international aid (Wintour, 2013). At a conference on tackling world hunger, he declared that he was proud of Britain's record on international aid and justified spending on the policy, stating that there is a 'moral case for keeping our promises to the world's poorest' and in 'doing what is right' (Cameron, 2013c). Yet, he also stated a more classically realist conservative case for such spending by declaring, 'We understand that if we invest in countries before they get broken we might not end up spending so much on dealing with the problems whether that's immigration or new threats to our national security' (ibid.).

DOI: 10.1057/9781137505781.0009

Spending on humanitarian aid was also justified by the benefits it can bring to British business. As a policy paper produced by the Department for International Development made clear:

> Promoting wealth and job creation in the poorest countries is not just morally right but it is in the UK's interests too. It is in the emerging markets that were poor just 10 or 20 years ago that UK companies are now winning new business and which are expanding at unprecedented rates. (2011, p. 7)

Humanitarian aid as a tool of soft power is thus seen to benefit foreign peoples, UK business and the British state. The first are thought to benefit from the increased prosperity brought by economic development. The second are thought to benefit from new investment opportunities, while the third may benefit from the moral capital to be gained from humanitarian intervention. A recent House of Lords report on soft power and the global influence of the United Kingdom thus highlighted the important role to be played by the Department for International Development (DFID) in the spread of British values and soft power throughout the world (House of Lords, 2014, para. 131, p. 75).

The benefits brought to British businesses from UK development aid are not the result of a happy coincidence, an accidental benefit of a value-based policy. For the British government, it would seem that market values and democratic values are conflated as a commitment to free trade and open markets is regarded as being intrinsic to the more general commitment to liberty. One of the aims of DFID is to encourage what it describes as 'good governance' which entails beating corruption but also establishing the rule of law *and* reduced trade barriers (Department for International Development, 2014). Democratic freedoms are inextricably linked to economic freedoms: 'open economies are reinforced by open societies....in which individual rights to liberty and property are safeguarded' (Greening, 2014). DFID has consequently funded programmes encouraging free trade and privatisation in the name of democracy and poverty reduction. It funds organisations such as the Westminster Consortium for Parliaments and Democracy which works in foreign countries to 'strengthen parliamentary democracy by building capacity in the areas of parliamentary process and management, financial oversight and access to information' (Westminster Foundation for Democracy, 2014). The consortium is led by the Westminster Foundation for Democracy, an

DOI: 10.1057/9781137505781.0009

organisation sponsored by the Foreign and Commonwealth Office. It aims to support 'good governance' and 'democratic practices' which in practice includes developing the institutional frameworks favourable to UK trade and investment. For example, in Uganda it was involved in the rewriting of legislation which allows the de facto privatisation of national oil reserves (Fisher, 2013, p. 342). Private consultancy firms are also beneficiaries of DFID aid, notably Adam Smith International which emerged from the right-wing think tank, the Adam Smith Institute, known for lobbying the Thatcher government for privatisation in the 1980s (*The Guardian*, 2012). The company was involved in advising the Iraqi government on the privatisation of water services following the British–American invasion (Adam Smith International, 2014; Whyte, 2007). British companies of course also benefit from increased investment opportunities once economies have been opened up to international trade.

The extent to which the corporate-friendly international development policies actually favour local peoples, notably by tackling poverty, is highly questionable. There is evidence to suggest that privatisation may exacerbate poverty by pushing up the costs of basic utilities such as water and electricity (Hilary, 2004). Economic development may also be hindered if local companies are pushed out of the market by increased competition from heavily subsidised British industries. In Bangladesh, the World Bank's Private Sector Development Support Project, partly funded by DFID, aims to encourage the development of more Special Economic Zones (SEZs) in which companies may benefit from favourable tax and regulatory regimes. Most of the companies are garment manufacturers making products for large multinationals. While the British government works to ensure that companies in SEZs comply with local labour laws, it is in favour of keeping wages no higher than the local minimum, ensuring that the zones remain attractive for foreign investors (Corporate Watch, 2011). As a result, local people are likely to remain trapped in poverty. The freedom of local countries is in practice limited to their ' "freedom" to embrace the rules, norms and principles of the emerging (neo)liberal global order' (Ayers, 2009).

Rather than empowering local people and achieving humanitarian objectives, it would appear that the Coalition's foreign policy is primarily driven by self-interest. Indeed, the replacement of William Hague at the Foreign Office by Philip Hammond seems to mark the return to a more overtly self-interested policy. In his first speech as foreign secretary to the Conservative Party conference, Hammond declared:

> I've told our diplomats that it might be called 'The Foreign Office', but I want them to think of it as 'The British Office'. Because their job is to bat for Britain: protecting our security; standing up for our values; and pursuing our prosperity, playing a vital role in the Conservative plan to secure a better future for Britain. (2014)

The key mission of British embassies throughout the world is 'to break open markets, attract new investment, boost British business and create British jobs' (ibid.). For Vickers, the increased emphasis on commercial objectives in foreign policy under the Coalition is what really distinguishes it from past policy (Vickers, 2011, p. 211). While such objectives have arguably always been central to foreign policy, perhaps it is the context of the current economic crisis and the fall of dictatorial regimes in the Middle East that has provided a new spur for an economic policy that may enable Britain to recapture its position as a key world power. Indeed, both Hague and Hammond shared the desire to demonstrate Britain's importance on the world stage.

Keen to avoid the mistakes of Iraq and to limit defence spending, soft power has become regarded as the best means by which to do this, although this does not preclude the use of hard power when absolutely necessary. While institutions such as embassies, the BBC and the British Council remain important in terms of spreading British cultural influence throughout the globe, corporations have become the key tools in the coalition government's drive to defend Britain's global position. As on the domestic scene, government and corporations have again formed a veritable coalition of interests as both seek to gain from the opening up of global markets. The British government can hope to gain from the moral capital conferred by 'humanitarian' development aid while also extending its influence across the globe via the British companies which represent it and its values. To a certain extent, this allows the United Kingdom to punch above its weight and to continue to exercise power over foreign nations in its own national interests. The language of liberalism and humanitarianism allows it to pursue a policy of 'liberal imperialism' but a more appropriate term to describe current policy may be that of 'corporate imperialism', highlighting the role of companies as a tool of soft power.

DOI: 10.1057/9781137505781.0009

Europe and soft power

The desire to protect corporate interests has also influenced the Coalition's policy towards Europe. Yet, such a concern is no longer masked by humanitarian discourse. While a commitment to human rights legitimised intervention overseas to empower local peoples, the European concern for human rights is presented as *disempowering* British people. Government opposition to EU membership is largely presented in populist terms, as a threat to British national sovereignty and democratic political accountability. Consequently, the Coalition has promised to allow the British people to have their say on the issue via referendum. The *European Union Act* passed in 2011 introduced a so-called 'referendum lock', preventing government from ceding more power to the European Union unless such a concession of power is approved in a referendum. Of course, the Conservatives have also pledged to hold a referendum in 2017 on European membership should they be re-elected in 2015.

Populist discourse on Europe also helps to satisfy Eurosceptic conservative backbenchers. They are significant in numerical terms and can only be ignored at the prime minister's peril. Backbench rebellions on Europe have been significant. The rebellion of October 2011 by backbench MPs demanding an immediate in–out referendum on Europe was quelled but it 'constituted the largest rebellion on the issue of Europe of the post-war era' (Cowley & Stuart, 2012, p. 402) and 'dwarfed the revolts of the 1990s' (Gamble, 2012b, p. 468). Cameron's subsequent commitment, made in January 2013, to hold an in–out referendum in 2017, and the appointment of Eurosceptic Philip Hammond as Foreign Secretary in July 2014, may be regarded partly as a response to backbench pressure. While Cameron's own Euroscepticism is regarded as having contributed to his leadership election victory in 2005 (Bale, 2010, pp. 264–9) and although he 'speaks a good sceptic talk' on Europe, 'his actions point in a different direction' (Gamble, 2012b, p. 475).

Cameron was described as a 'mild Eurosceptic' in Opposition (Lynch, 2009, p. 187). While his Euroscepticism has hardened (Lynch, 2011, p. 222), especially in the face of electoral threats from the hard Eurosceptic United Kingdom Independence Party (UKIP), he remains committed to Europe. As he made clear in his 2013 speech promising a 2017 referendum, his principal aim is to reform Europe, not withdraw from it. Indeed, he ended his speech by highlighting his desire for Britain to remain in Europe, stating, 'I believe in something very deeply. That

DOI: 10.1057/9781137505781.0009

Britain's national interest is best served in a flexible, adaptable and open European Union and that such a European Union is best with Britain in it' (2013d). For Cameron, that national interest is best served when British business interests are protected: ensuring that they are has played a key role in Britain's approach to the European Union since it joined. European policy under the Coalition is thus wholly coherent with its foreign policy objectives more generally.

The government has adopted both 'hard' and 'soft' approaches to ensuring that Britain gets her way in Europe. The former approach was adopted by the prime minister in December 2011 when he vetoed the Franco-German deal to impose sanctions on EU countries which break the Euro's debt and deficit rule. Threats to withdraw from the European Union, should British demands for reform not be met, may also be considered as a similar tactic. Yet, soft power has also been deployed as more subtle means of influencing EU policy have continued. With regard to securing Britain's economic interests, the United Kingdom was influential in creating the single market and it continues to push for the completion of that market in the energy, digital and service sectors of the economy. Under Cameron, the government set itself three specific aims concerning EU economic policy: reducing the European Union's budget; initiating negotiations with the United States on an EU–US trade agreement; and opposing a financial transactions tax (British Influence, 2014, p. 25). According to the think-tank 'British Influence', the government has been quite successful in achieving these goals (ibid., 2014). In February 2013, the UK government, supported by German and Dutch allies, helped to secure a cut in the EU budget in real terms for the financial period 2014–20, although it failed to achieve its objective of reducing administrative costs and targeting spending primarily on jobs and growth (ibid., pp. 25–8). It was also successful in terms of securing its objective of opening talks between the European Union and the United States on the Transatlantic Trade and Investment Partnership, although at the time of writing no agreement has yet been signed (ibid., p. 29). The UK government has perhaps been less successful in opposing an EU-wide financial transactions tax: the plan has now been dropped but other EU member states are planning to adopt such a measure individually (ibid., p. 30).

It is of course difficult to measure with any precision the influence that the British government has had in negotiations over these policy areas but it is certainly well-placed to make its influence felt. Apart from being

DOI: 10.1057/9781137505781.0009

able to exercise influence via formal voting procedures (with the third largest share of votes after Germany and France), the United Kingdom possesses a number of informal tools of influence (CBI, 2013, pp. 97–8). It is good at building alliances with other member states to exert pressure over key policies (ibid., pp. 99–101). It is reputed for having specific technical expertise, notably on financial services, which may help it to influence legislation in that area (ibid., pp. 104–5). Its role in global institutions such as the World Trade Organisation (WTO) may enable it to exert international pressure on the European Union (ibid., pp. 105–7). Finally, British citizens occupy key positions across EU institutions (ibid., pp. 102–3). Many of these individuals have links to the financial industry, such as Jonathan Hill, a former lobbyist for the financial sector, who occupies the post of Commissioner for financial markets (Corporate Europe Observatory, 2014a).

While the direct influence of British government may be important in enabling it to exercise soft power, the influence of corporations and their lobbies is also essential. Indeed, British companies, trade associations, consultancies, law firms and think tanks engaged in lobbying activity in Brussels are massively over-represented compared to those from other member states (Tansey, 2012). The UK financial lobby is particularly active in Brussels, with British financial industry firms outnumbering all other such organisations from across the European Union (Corporate Europe Observatory, 2014b, pp. 10–12). The precise influence of these groups on policy development is certainly difficult to measure but it would be rather surprising if their influence was not at least partly in proportion to their numerical and financial strength. It is estimated that the financial industry lobby consists of five times more entities than NGOs, trade unions and consumer organisations together and out-spends the latter by a ratio of at least 30:1 when it comes to lobbying activity (ibid., pp. 10–14). Furthermore, the financial industry lobby dominates 'Expert Groups' who are the primary advisers to the European Commission on financial regulation (Alliance for Lobbying Transparency and Ethics Regulation, 2009). Perhaps this helps to explain why European measures on financial regulation have so far been very weak: most notably, the European Commission has, like the United Kingdom, shied away from imposing full structural separation of retail and investment banking activities (Wahl, 2014).

Large corporations and the financial sector appear to be essential to the effective exercise of British soft power in Europe, as elsewhere in

DOI: 10.1057/9781137505781.0009

the world. Shaping European policy in favour of business interests is of direct benefit to the British government, particularly a Conservative government, that can proudly claim to have played a significant part in the creation of 'a more flexible, adaptable and open European Union' (Cameron, 2013d). Britain can then be seen to be leading Europe, not subservient to it, leading 'the charge in the fight for global trade and against protectionism' (ibid.).

Once again, despite the populist discourse about EU reform being in the best interests of the British people, policy in this area may actually run counter to their interests. Rather than empowering the British people, the creation of 'a more flexible, adaptable and open European Union' may actually disempower them. For example, the key reform to this end under negotiation at the time of writing – the Transatlantic Trade and Investment Partnership (TTIP) – may move decision-making even further away from citizens in member countries. They already feel far-removed from negotiations in Brussels, but at least they have the right to elect representatives to the European Parliament. Under the TTIP, decisions which may affect them could be taken at a supranational level between the European Union and unelected representatives from the United States. The free trade agreement is likely to include investor-state dispute settlement mechanisms, effectively enabling companies to sue elected governments if they adopt policies which, while in the public interest, limit their profit margins (Corporate Europe Observatory, 2014c). In practice, corporations are empowered at the expense of ordinary citizens, despite the Coalition's discourse on popular sovereignty, while the soft power of the State is in no way diminished. This is true both within the United Kingdom and abroad.

DOI: 10.1057/9781137505781.0009

6

Solving the Paradox of Liberal Politics

Abstract: *This chapter attempts to understand the paradox of liberal politics under the coalition in Britain. It begins by attempting to situate liberal authoritarianism in conservative and liberal traditions. It then looks at the role played by statecraft, asking if liberal authoritarianism has been motivated less by ideology and more by a simple desire to stay in power. The coalition strategy is viewed in light of the statecraft of neoliberal governmentality, as a way of shifting responsibility onto individuals, making them more 'free' to govern their own lives and take their own decisions, through coercive means if necessary. A brief look at neoliberal theory demonstrates how state coercion in some spheres has always been deemed acceptable in the name of a narrow conception of freedom.*

Keywords: liberal authoritarianism; neoliberal governmentality; statecraft

Bell, Emma. *Soft Power and Freedom under the Coalition: State-Corporate Power and the Threat to Democracy.* Basingstoke: Palgrave Macmillan, 2015. DOI: 10.1057/9781137505781.0010.

The Coalition has been described as 'a tale of two liberalisms' (Beech, 2011a). This suggests that although the Coalition may at first sight appear to be an alliance of two very different kinds of liberalism, one promoting social liberalism and the other economic, in reality both have come to embrace economic liberalism, just as both have come to support *certain forms* of moral liberalism (at least at the level of leadership, if not the grassroots). The principal aim of both parties has been to reduce the role of the State in the resolution of social and economic problems, thus supposedly liberating individuals and communities. Yet, as the above exploration of key policies designed to promote 'liberalism' has shown, these ostensibly 'liberal' parties have together pursued policies which have actually *extended* the power and the reach of the State, resulting in liberal authoritarianism. Indeed, policies have not been overtly authoritarian, but rather sought to engineer change via more subtle means, often using the private sector as an instrument of 'soft power'. The result has been the disempowerment of civil society.

This chapter attempts to understand this paradox of liberal politics under the coalition in Britain, namely why liberalism has failed to guarantee the freedom of the British people. It begins by situating liberal authoritarianism in the tradition of the Conservative Party, noting that these contradictory tendencies have always been present. It then asks if these trends may be seen to sit well with the tradition of the Liberal Democrats. The chapter moves on to look at the role played by statecraft, asking if liberal authoritarianism has been motivated less by ideology and more by a simple desire to stay in power and hold the coalition together. Certainly, liberal discourse was important for the Conservative Party as a means of 'detoxifying' the party and helping it to shed its 'nasty party' image. Similarly, the strand of moral authoritarianism that has been directed towards the most vulnerable groups in the population has arguably helped to secure electoral support given the lack of public sympathy for these groups, notably the poor and immigrants. The strategy of deresponsibilisation of the state mentioned earlier can also be seen as a good legitimation strategy. Indeed, this may be regarded as the statecraft of neoliberal governmentality, as a way of shifting responsibility onto individuals, making them more 'free' to govern their own lives and take their own decisions, through coercive means if necessary. A brief look at neoliberal theory demonstrates how state coercion in some spheres has always been deemed acceptable in the name of a narrow conception of freedom.

DOI: 10.1057/9781137505781.0010

Liberal authoritarianism in the conservative tradition

The traditional tension in the Conservative Party between its authoritarian and liberal traditions continued under the leadership of David Cameron (Alexandre-Collier, 2010). But while there may often be tension between the two, both are regarded as being essential to the party. Liam Fox, a former Conservative Party Chairman and Minister of State, claimed that liberty and authority are 'the twin pillars of conservatism' (Fox, 2004). They are not necessarily contradictory ideas but may in fact complement each other. Indeed, key conservative thinkers such as Roger Scruton believe that liberty must be bounded by authority (Barry, 2005, p. 33). This was evident under Margaret Thatcher whose policies entailed boosting state authority and limiting certain freedoms in order to drive through her free market reforms. Authoritarian policies towards those who interfered with the functioning of the free market, notably striking miners, were justified as facilitating the pursuit of liberty. A liberal economy would, she argued, free citizens from dependency on the State and give them more control over their own lives. Her apparently contradictory strategy was famously summarised as 'the free economy and the strong state' (Gamble, 1994). Yet, if the economy was liberalised, the role of the State was not necessarily reduced as government continued to intervene to support the economy by providing various forms of welfare to corporations.

The anti-statist rhetoric adopted by the Thatcher governments and her followers since does not fit well with conservative tradition. Indeed, until the 1970s, the Conservatives had believed in an important role for the state in economic planning and were, with few exceptions, opposed to *laissez-faire* (Green, 2002, pp. 241–56). Their aim was to strike the right balance between the latter and socialist state interventionism. While the 1980s seemed to mark a break from that tradition with the Thatcher governments' reiteration of anti-statist rhetoric, in practice there was still a significant role for the State. Indeed, as Green explains, Conservatives have only ever been prepared to retreat from the State when they believe that the agencies of civil society are fit to step in to assure the order and cohesiveness of society. When they regard the latter as ineffective, they accept state intervention as necessary (ibid., p. 241). This was perhaps considered to be especially necessary at a time when the government considered that a profound cultural change was required within civil society to eliminate the so-called dependency culture. It should be noted

DOI: 10.1057/9781137505781.0010

that political concerns have also played a role in Conservative decisions to retreat from the State, such as during the Thatcher years when reducing the role of the State in the NHS was considered to be too unpopular among the public to make fundamental reform possible.

With their 'Big Society' discourse, Cameron's Conservatives may perhaps be regarded as having more faith in the effectiveness of civil society and therefore be more likely to fall back less on authority and the State. Indeed, solving social problems from 'the bottom up' seems to be a much more liberal approach than enforcing solutions from the 'top down'. It has been described as 'civic conservatism' (Willets, 1994) or 'compassionate conservatism' (Willets, 2005; Norman & Ganesh, 2006). It entails recognising the importance of society and the 'interconnectedness' we have with other people. It is about developing a 'neighbourly society' 'built upon strong and supportive relationships within families, between neighbours and throughout the wider community' in which people get together to tackle social problems such as poverty and even the causes of crime (Letwin, 2002b). The State should not attempt to enforce grand plans on civil society but content itself to provide the framework of rules and laws necessary to enable society to function correctly. This would appear to be the kind of ideal society that Cameron had in mind when promoting the 'Big Society': the State would take a step back and allow individuals and communities to come up with local solutions to local problems.

Yet, as demonstrated earlier, the State retained a significant directive role, for example, enforcing sanctions on those who are not seen to act as sufficiently responsible members of civil society. The State thus does more than simply providing the framework in which civil society can function correctly. Despite having embraced 'nudge theory' according to which people can be gently encouraged to change their behaviour via various unobtrusive interventions which are intended to be more effective than coercion or regulation (Thaler and Sunstein, 2008), the Conservative-led coalition has in reality been rather coercive when it comes to getting people involved in the 'Big Society', most notably as responsible workers.

Furthermore, the Coalition's view of civil society is one which includes not just individuals and communities but also private companies who are to work in partnership towards the resolution of social problems. This view supposes that they are all equal actors in civil society but in practice

DOI: 10.1057/9781137505781.0010

the private sector has considerably more power. As highlighted earlier, it can no longer be regarded as being part of civil society but rather as part of government itself. As such, it plays a significant role in extending the power of the state through civil society, in some cases even determining who may or may not have access to the rights of citizenship.

In practice, it would seem that the Conservatives in government under Cameron went much further than the tradition of 'civic conservatism' allows. Yet, in doing so it might be argued that they were simply falling back on their tradition of authoritarianism. Indeed, authoritarianism and liberalism are extremely difficult to balance, a point recognised by the neoliberal philosopher Hayek who cited the conservative 'fondness for authority' as a principal reason why he could not consider himself as a conservative (Hayek in Hamowy, 2011, p. 522). Far from being radical, the project of 'civic conservatism' or 'compassionate conservatism' which seeks to limit the State and restore the freedom of ordinary people, may perhaps be regarded as reactionary. The term is not intended to be pejorative – indeed it is one that is adopted by many Conservatives themselves. It serves to underline the fact that Conservatives are naturally disinclined to go against tradition (King, 2011).

The policies adopted by Cameron's Conservatives in government may thus be understood as fitting with that tradition, rather than as being something genuinely new. The policies of localism are as much a reaction against the authoritarian policies of the New Labour government as they are a genuine commitment to liberalism. They are also a reaction against social democracy, reflecting a desire to return to a time when people did not look to the State to solve their problems. While the rhetoric adopted is progressive, the aim is to defend tradition. As is common to Conservatives, radical methods may even be employed in the defence of tradition (Robin, 2011, pp. 48–57). Indeed, Thatcher famously described herself as a 'conservative revolutionary' (Thatcher, 1992) and justified the adoption of radical methods in the pursuit of conservative aims. Cameron too adopts the language of progress and revolution, promising a 'rehabilitation revolution', a 'revolution in public services' and 'a devolution revolution', for example. Yet, while many of these policies mark a break from the recent past, in many ways they represent a return to a more distant past, particularly public service reform which seeks to totally reverse the social democratic postwar consensus. Contemporary conservative policies are thus more 'restorationist' than they are radical,

DOI: 10.1057/9781137505781.0010

revolutionary or progressive – they seek to restore the conditions of the past. Current economic policy is a case in point: despite the rhetoric of renewal and the transformation of capitalism, policy has in practice been geared towards restoring 'the conditions for "business as usual"' (Clarke, 2012, p. 49). Furthermore, despite the popular connotations associated with the language of revolution, the project is to be led from above, using authoritarian methods where necessary to crush resistance.

Liberal authoritarianism and the Liberal Democrats

While the current tension between authoritarianism and liberalism seems to fit well with conservative tradition, it would seem to be much less at ease with the traditions of the Liberal Democrats. Indeed, it is a commitment to liberty that has defined the party through its various transformations, from the Whigs of the seventeenth century through to the modern Liberal Democrat Party today. In its beginnings, the party was reputed for its commitment to political liberalism, associated with the writings of John Locke, and today still prides itself on its defence of civil liberties. In the nineteenth century, the party was most commonly associated with economic liberalism although it was also committed to the spread of democracy via the extension of the franchise. In the early twentieth century, it came to accept the need for a limited role for the state in order to free people from poverty, leading the government of Asquith to lay the foundations for Britain's welfare state. The party's commitment to social liberalism has been evident in recent years in its defence of gay rights. It is this latter form of liberalism which has proved most unpalatable to some of its conservative partners in the Coalition, symbolised by the fact that more conservative MPs voted against the *Marriage (Same Sex Couples Act) 2013* than those who voted in favour. Senior Liberal Democrats have also found some conservative policies unpalatable, particularly those that seem to threaten civil liberties, most notably the commitment to repeal the *Human Rights Act*.

Yet, in the past, liberal thought also contained an element of authoritarianism with the key New Liberal thinker, Leonard Trelawny Hobhouse, suggesting that every freedom should rest upon a corresponding act of control (Rose, 1999, p. 120). The liberals of the time (along with many socialists) saw a significant role for the State to engineer a better society.

DOI: 10.1057/9781137505781.0010

This could imply 'stern repression of the unfit, plus positive eugenic measures for environmental and hygienic improvements in the interest of social progress' (ibid., p. 116).

Contemporary Liberals also accept the duality of freedom and control. It would seem that there was a consensus within the coalition, not just on the need to restore liberty to individuals and communities by rolling back the state, but also, perhaps paradoxically, on policies which pose a threat to liberty. Despite presenting themselves as the party best placed to defend civil liberties, proudly claiming to have scrapped New Labour's ID card scheme, ended the storing of the DNA of innocent people for an indeterminate period of time and restored the right to protest outside Parliament (Liberal Democrats, 2014), the Liberal Democrats in government failed to oppose conservative legislation which may threaten basic freedoms. For example, all but two Liberal Democrats present in the House of Commons on the day of the division on the final reading on the Data Retention and Investigatory Powers Bill voted in favour of the new law which threatens the right to privacy of British citizens. Liberal Democrat MPs also supported the government's anti-terror legislation, notably permitting the detention of terrorist suspects for up to 14 days. Furthermore, they failed to retain basic legal protections; while Liberal Democrat peers opposed the government's cuts to legal aid under the *Legal Aid, Sentencing and Punishment of Offenders Act 2012*, these were supported by Liberal Democrat MPs.

It might be suggested that Liberal Democrat MPs were forced into compromise by their stronger Conservative partners in government. Indeed, we have highlighted a number of conservative 'red-line' issues, on Europe, immigration and the economy, over which the Liberal Democrats had virtually no influence. In this respect, the practice of coalition government 'shows what happens when vegetarians negotiate with carnivores' (Bale, 2012, p. 328), suggesting that the Liberal Democrats have had to renounce some of their core beliefs and give in to the Conservatives. Hall suggested that the Liberal Democrats served as a mere fig leaf, helping to give an acceptable face to the more radical aspects of conservative policy (2012, p. 22). Indeed, there are very few areas in government where the Liberal Democrats seem to have got their way, even if rebellion, particularly from the backbenches, has been vocal at times.

Yet, there are some areas where the Liberal Democrats were active supporters of conservative policies. For those wishing to 'reclaim' the

DOI: 10.1057/9781137505781.0010

party's 'liberal heritage' and reduce the role of the state, it is necessary to place its commitment to economic liberalism in the foreground (Laws, 2012). This concern largely reflects that of the authors of *The Orange Book* (Marshall & Laws, 2004) in which senior party members attempted to trace a new direction for the party. David Laws, one of the chief negotiators of the coalition agreement, suggests that it is not just a conservative agenda that was delivered by the Coalition in government but also the agenda laid out in the *Orange Book* (Laws, 2012). Indeed, deficit reduction and the reform of public services were key ideas initially traced by the party back in 2004. The idea of free schools, the encouragement of private pension funds, the introduction of more private providers into the NHS and the privatisation of Royal Mail were all ideas mooted by the Liberal Democrats before the Coalition was even formed. There was, importantly, a strong commitment to reducing the role of the state by involving the private and third sectors in public service delivery. Yet, as illustrated in the preceding chapters, in practice this has not led to a reduction of state power in favour of individuals and local communities who are actually rendered less free by the increasing power of unelected representatives from the private sector. So, while there may be no clear authoritarian tradition in the Liberal Democrat Party, unlike in the Conservative Party, the unleashing of the power of the private sector has made it very difficult for the Liberal Democrats to defend the freedoms of individuals. While the principal difficulty of the Conservatives has been reconciling liberty and authority, the chief difficulty of the Liberal Democrats has been balancing the four freedoms identified in *The Orange Book* as being at the heart of their agenda: political, personal, social and economic freedom. Once this latter freedom takes precedence, the other freedoms are put at risk: political freedom is threatened by the disproportionate influence of the private sector on government decision-making; personal freedom is limited by the widespread surveillance of the state in partnership with private companies; social freedom is threatened by the privatisation of public services which undermines the principle of universality and deliberately excludes some citizens from access to welfare.

The statecraft of neoliberal governmentality

While important, party ideology alone cannot provide a satisfactory explanation for current authoritarian trends. Indeed, ideology itself is

DOI: 10.1057/9781137505781.0010

influenced by more practical concerns, notably the practical exigencies of statecraft, and vice versa (Hayton, 2014). The Conservative Party in particular, as an essentially pragmatic party more concerned with winning power than following ideology, has often been associated with the practice of statecraft, defined by Bulpitt as 'the art of winning elections and, above all, achieving a necessary degree of governing competence in office' (Bulpitt, 1986, p. 19). Yet, the Liberal Democrats, cast out of power for so long, have also been prepared to exercise statecraft in an attempt to make themselves electable and to share power with their traditional opponents. Liberalism as a tool of statecraft is perhaps more easily explained than authoritarianism. Liberal discourse was an important way for the Liberal Democrats to remind voters that they are the traditional party of civil liberties, thus marking themselves out from New Labour who had stolen many of their clothes in the mid-1990s. Their discourse on the shrinking of the State was also a way of making the party more palatable to the Conservatives as coalition partners, even though this was developed by *The Orange Book* supporters in the party long before the possibility of a Conservative–Liberal Democrat coalition could even be contemplated. For the Conservatives, liberal discourse allowed them to distinguish themselves from both New Labour and its questionable record on civil liberties and from the moral conservatism of the Thatcher years (Alexandre-Collier, 2010, p. 27). Even liberal discourse on the economy can be seen as a form of statecraft, enabling the Conservatives to blame the financial crisis on their political predecessors and thus assume the mantle of the party to be most trusted with economic management (Gamble, 2014).

While authoritarianism under the Coalition was generally hidden behind liberalism, some aspects of it were openly flaunted. The government was not shy about adopting coercive policies with regard to certain groups of people, notably 'undeserving' welfare claimants, migrants and suspected terrorists. The financial crisis, for example, was not presented as a crisis of the neoliberal economic model or as one caused by the bankers but as a crisis of the welfare state, fuelled by increased spending on migrants and 'scroungers'. Like the New Labour government before it, it exploited popular fears about external and internal threats to economic, physical and social security, identifying suitable scapegoats and promising to reassert its regalian powers in order to deal with them.

DOI: 10.1057/9781137505781.0010

As statecraft, such a strategy enabled the government to boost its own popularity by tapping into popular fears and prejudices. While the Coalition helped construct the narrative that welfare spending was too high, it was also responding to a popular belief that this was the case (YouGov, 2012; Clery et al., 2013). Similarly, the Coalition's authoritarian immigration policies tap into a popular consensus that immigration is a problem and ought to be reduced (NatCen, 2013). Although it is impossible to measure the impact of government policies on public attitudes, it is entirely possible that they may help to reinforce certain beliefs among the public by presenting them as mainstream and legitimate. As Stuart Hall pointed out some time ago, policies which play on popular fears are not just populist but authoritarian populist – they are imposed from above but appear to come from 'below' (1988). This is how states create hegemony in the Gramscian sense of the term: they do not just respond to popular fears with authoritarian policies; their response is in itself authoritarian to the extent that it precludes genuine public debate about certain subjects, thus disempowering the public as a whole. Yet, it enables the State to appear to be responding to the citizenry and also to reassert its regalian functions, proving its usefulness to the public. This has paradoxically become all the more important as the State has declared itself powerless in the face of mounting social problems. Rather than state solutions, the Coalition has encouraged members of the 'Big Society' to find their own solutions to these problems. Yet, it still needs to show that it can step in where necessary, forcing individuals to become responsible. At the same time, the public gaze is directed downwards towards the 'irresponsible' and away from the elites whose policies may be thought to have caused certain problems. The latter are effectively deresponsibilised.

Such a strategy may be interpreted as liberal statecraft: the power of the State is legitimated by its commitment to limit and share that power with other actors in civil society. Yet, while appearing to relinquish power, it is in fact using it in more subtle ways to encourage people to become responsible, self-governing individuals – for Foucault, this was the essence of liberal governmentality (Foucault, 1979 in Senellart, 2008). Liberty is not an end in itself but is rather seen as a *strategy* of government, a form of statecraft, enabling the State to govern more effectively (Dean, 2010). It is a means of legitimising government intervention to 'discipline' those who fail to act responsibly. This has become all the more important under neoliberal forms of capitalism: as the State has retreated

DOI: 10.1057/9781137505781.0010

from the provision of social and economic security for its citizens, they must be trained to provide this for themselves. Those who fail to do so must be seen as personally responsible for this failure, justifying coercive measures against them while shielding the State from blame.

Liberty must be directed from above. The freedom of some cannot be permitted to interfere with that of others, to follow J. S. Mill's 'harm principle' (Mill, 1869). The State can legitimate draconian anti-terror measures and mass surveillance in order to protect the freedom and the security of the masses. It can also legitimate limiting the freedoms of individuals and communities to take their own decisions when these conflict with national policy. For example, locally agreed planning decisions cannot be permitted to interfere with national planning, just as independent 'free schools' must respect directives laid down by central government. The State's role is to manage freedom.

This is not to suggest that 'freedom is a sham' but simply to suggest that freedom needs to be understood as a more complex phenomenon than may be thought: 'it is to say that the agonistic relation between liberty and government is an intrinsic part of what we have come to know as freedom' (Rose, 1996, pp. 61–2). We should not assume that freedom precludes authoritarianism and state coercion but accept that both concepts may work in symbiosis with one another. Liberal government may use freedom for its own ends but that does not mean that its aim is to render the citizenry less free. It does not, however, follow that we should not be concerned about how government uses freedom as a tool of statecraft. As seen with the example of Britain's coalition government, the language of freedom can blind us to the fact that citizens are sometimes disempowered by certain policies.

Most importantly, a discourse that emphasises the freedom of individuals over the power of the State often diverts attention away from the other actors involved in exercising power on behalf of the State by creating a false dichotomy between individual and state power. This points to a key distinction between liberal governmentality as statecraft and *neo*liberal governmentality as statecraft. Following the former strategy, the State exercised power through a wide variety of state-appointed experts – social workers, teachers, probation officers and so on – while under the latter, the State has come to exercise power increasingly through a range of entirely private actors. While state-appointed actors in governance were directly accountable to the people, this is no longer the case with private actors who are only accountable to the State itself, making it

DOI: 10.1057/9781137505781.0010

harder for citizens to protect their freedoms. Furthermore, private actors wield significantly more power than their public-sector counterparts, as veritable partners in government. Yet, they are not guided by an ethos of public service but rather by the self-interest of profit. The Coalition's introduction of payment-by-results for private providers of public services implies recognition of this fact. Economic incentives aim to ensure that they will act as directed by the State, implementing (often coercive) policy from the centre while remaining ostensibly independent. Yet, they are often involved in policymaking themselves, meaning that state power and that of the private sector becomes mutually reinforcing. Meanwhile, the power of individuals is further weakened, highlighting the contradiction central to the practice of neoliberal statecraft. Yet, it is a contradiction that works well in terms of statecraft. As Hall has suggested, 'ideology works best by suturing together contradictory lines of argument' (Hall, 2012, p. 17).

Neoliberal ideology and authoritarianism

It is the contradiction between liberalism and authoritarianism central to conservative and even liberal thought that makes it such an effective tool of statecraft, allowing the government to deploy liberal and authoritarian methods simultaneously to legitimise neoliberal policies. Interestingly, neoliberal ideology itself also embodies a contradiction between liberalism and authoritarianism which might also explain why the policies of the coalition government have not marked a distinct departure from the New Labour years, despite some differences of emphasis. While there are of course many varieties of neoliberalism, one common feature would seem to be an 'affinity between free-market economics and authoritarian politics' (Scheuerman, 1999, p. 224). This is certainly evidenced in Britain since at least the 1980s onwards, whatever government has been in power. The Thatcher governments used the full authority of the State to ensure that workers could not interfere with the functioning of the 'free' economy, whether by limiting trade union rights or deregulating the workplace, by force if necessary. The Blair governments retained strict trade union legislation and further extended workplace deregulation. Similarly, as we have seen, the Cameron-led coalition has used coercive methods to ensure that the power of ordinary citizens can in no way interfere with the power of the market. While they were probably not directly inspired

DOI: 10.1057/9781137505781.0010

by neoliberal theory, there is striking resemblance between contemporary social and economic policy and that promoted by early neoliberal thinkers, notably the ordoliberals of the Freiburg school, who believed that economic freedom can only derive from a strong state.

For the ordoliberals, the role of the State was to preserve the freedom of the entrepreneur above all other freedoms (Bonefeld, 2012). While economic policy is to be directed at freeing up the market as far as possible, social policy is to be aimed at restoring the *vitalpolitik*, as explained in Chapter 2. A strong state is needed to order economic freedom to prevent the development of monopolies, for example, that may hinder the functioning of the free market. This is what distinguished the ordoliberals – or the neoliberals, as some of them called themselves – from the classical liberals of the nineteenth century who favoured the 'night-watchman state'. This would suggest that there is no contradiction between contemporary market intervention and a belief in economic liberalism, provided that the former is justified by the protection of the freedom of the entrepreneur. David Cameron shares such a belief, stating, 'No true Conservative has a naive belief that all politics has to do is step back and let capitalism rip' (2012b). Yet, he also declared, 'While of course there is a role for government, for regulation and intervention, the real solution is more enterprise, competition and innovation' (ibid.).

This belief that government should encourage competition was also shared by the ordoliberals. Indeed, for them, a strong state was required to 'liberate' workers from the welfare state, using coercive methods if necessary to turn them into 'entrepreneur[s] of labour power endowed with firm social and ethical values, and roots in tradition, family, and community' (Bonefeld, 2012, p. 643). This sums up the principal aim of the Coalition's social policy – to create responsible, free individuals capable of fending for themselves and finding work on the free market. Like the New Labour governments before it, and the Thatcher and Major governments before that, it aims to effect cultural change in order to foster the entrepreneurial spirit. Yet, it also seeks to anchor that culture in a new social order capable of replacing the welfare state, namely the 'Big Society'.

The creation of a new *vitalpolitik* may also be regarded as an effective tool of statecraft, allowing 'liberal' governments to create a new neoliberal culture supportive of neoliberal economic policies which prioritise negative freedoms from state interference over positive freedoms from

DOI: 10.1057/9781137505781.0010

poverty. While welfare is linked with dependency and unfreedom, entre-preneurialism is linked with freedom. Restoring responsibility to independent individuals means rendering them free of the State. It would indeed seem that neoliberal culture has been absorbed to a significant extent in the United Kingdom. The British Social Attitude Survey from 2012, comparing data from the survey first began in 1983, reveals:

> While attitudes to different aspects of welfare are behaving in a far from uniform way, they are generally moving in line with the current direction of government policy, rather than responding as they have previously to the onset of recession. We see that the public is becoming less supportive of the government taking a leading role in providing welfare to the unemployed, and even to the elderly in retirement. There is less enthusiasm about public spending on all types of benefits and an increasing belief that the welfare system encourages dependence. (Park et al., 2012, p. 17)

There are perhaps a number of reasons for increased punitiveness towards welfare claimants, for instance the decline in middle-class security which may make these classes more resentful of those at the bottom who are seen as the beneficiaries of unjust rewards (Young, 1999, pp. 8–10). But it may be that changing attitudes to welfare are also a manifestation of authoritarian populism at work whereby apparently 'popular' attitudes are partly moulded and led by the government itself. It is indeed surprising in the wake of a financial crisis caused by the incompetence and greed of those at the top of the social scale that vitriol continues to be directed predominantly downwards towards the poor and excluded rather than upwards to the economic elites. It would seem that a neoliberal culture has taken hold whereby 'egotistical individualism' is favoured over the 'reciprocal individualism' that characterised the years of postwar consensus (Reiner, 2007, p. 18). It is a form of individualism which negates the idea of collective responsibility in favour of one which promotes individual responsibility. It promotes 'competitive individualism' whereby individuals are encouraged to compete 'ruthlessly for rewards, thus encouraging initiative, enterprise and self-reliance among the competitors' (Gilbert, 2013b, pp. 30–1).

A culture of competitive individualism undermines the collective, weakening solidarity and the social movements which may emerge from it. This is not an unfortunate product of neoliberal culture but indeed its very *raison d'être*. The declared aim of the ordoliberals was the bounding of democracy to ensure that the sovereignty of the demos could not

DOI: 10.1057/9781137505781.0010

replace the sovereignty of the rule of law (Bonefeld, 2012, p. 636). They feared that organised interest groups lobbying government in favour of the masses would lead to group-specific legislation being passed that could hinder the freedom of the entrepreneur. As we noted in Chapter 4, selfish interest groups *do* influence government in contemporary society but they tend to be those promoting entrepreneurialism and their presence is therefore deemed acceptable. Protecting economic freedom is deliberately anti-democratic, aiming to prevent the masses from interfering in the processes of government, the primary aim of which is to restore power to the economic elites who were marginalised with the coming of twentieth-century democracy (Harvey, 2007). Yet, such a strategy is dressed in the language of liberalism. As the German conservative jurist and Nazi Carl Schmitt argued, putting down interest groups, by force if necessary, was the only way to restore the liberal rule of law which is regarded as inherently neutral (Scheuerman, 1999). These ideas were congenial to Hayek (ibid.) and seemed to be influential on Thatcher who often cited the need to uphold the rule of law as justification for limiting the power of the trade unions.

The undermining of the collective in favour of private capital is masked by the liberal discourse of the Coalition. It has focused not so much on the need to uphold the liberal rule of law but more on the capacity of private enterprise to free the individual. For David Cameron, it is private enterprise, not welfare, that is in the best interests of the individual. He declared:

> I believe that open markets and free enterprise are the best imaginable force for improving human wealth and happiness. They are the engine of progress, generating the enterprise and innovation that lifts people out of poverty and gives people opportunity. And I would go further: where they work properly, open markets and free enterprise can actually promote morality. Why? Because they create a direct link between contribution and reward; between effort and outcome. The fundamental basis of the market is the idea of something for something – an idea we need to encourage, not condemn. (2012b)

Rather than working against the collective, it is free enterprise that is thus presented as binding society together by linking the values of business to those of individuals and communities. Their values are in symbiosis, not in conflict. What is good for business is good for the community. The masses do not feel that their demands are being ignored since these are

DOI: 10.1057/9781137505781.0010

no longer seen as being fundamentally different from those of the free entrepreneur. As a strategy of neoliberal statecraft, this is particularly effective, helping to mask the antidemocratic nature of contemporary decision-making. It is the neoliberal commitment to the freedom of the private sector above that of ordinary citizens that lies at the heart of the paradox of liberal politics.

DOI: 10.1057/9781137505781.0010

Conclusion: New Directions for Liberalism?

Bell, Emma. *Soft Power and Freedom under the Coalition: State-Corporate Power and the Threat to Democracy.* Basingstoke: Palgrave Macmillan, 2015. DOI: 10.1057/9781137505781.0011.

▶

During its five years in power, the Conservative–Liberal Democrat coalition government worked, as promised, to restore freedom to the British people. Yet, freedom was understood in very narrow terms and the methods used to deliver it were often coercive in nature. Restoring freedoms to local communities entailed encouraging them to compete on the market with public and private providers to gain control over public services. Individuals were to be made free by encouraging them to change their values to become more competitive in the workplace. Ordinary citizens were to be set free from authoritarian measures that threatened their civil liberties but were in practice subject to widespread suspicionless surveillance. Austerity measures, while difficult to bear in the short term, were to free individuals from 'big government'. British people were to be freed from the diktat of the European Union while foreign peoples were to be freed from dictatorial regimes. Freedom was essentially understood in negative terms as freedom *from* the State to take responsibility for tackling local problems, finding employment, fighting crime and tackling the deficit.

Yet, as this analysis of different policy areas has demonstrated, responsibility did not necessarily equate with empowerment since central government continued to exercise a significant degree of control. In some cases, it did so directly, adopting quite openly coercive policies towards groups who tend to elicit little sympathy from the majority of the population, namely welfare claimants, immigrants and terrorist suspects. But intervention was often dressed up in the language of liberalism: it was about freeing people from poverty or getting ethnic minorities to accept the 'liberal' values of British society. On many occasions, state authoritarianism was operated via the intermediary of the private sector, rendering it more subtle and diffuse, as in the case of British corporations spreading soft power abroad. Consequently, rather than diluting the power of the State, partnership with the private sector has strengthened it. Perhaps the most striking illustration of soft power at work is the way in which governments since the 1980s onwards have succeeded in building a new hegemonic consensus around neoliberalism, underpinned by the spread of neoliberal culture.

While the real power of individuals has diminished, that of the private sector has increased. It is no longer regarded as one actor in civil society among others but has been accorded special citizenship status while also becoming a genuine partner in policymaking. As such, it has been granted significant freedom to pursue its own interests within a liberal

DOI: 10.1057/9781137505781.0011

framework of minimal regulation. Government has been prepared to limit the freedom of the market (largely via corporate welfare schemes) to ensure that the freedom of private enterprise is protected above all others. Given the fact that government is often judged on its ability to improve economic performance, this is also a good way to boost its own electoral popularity, especially as neoliberal hegemony works to equate the freedom of entrepreneurs with that of individuals.

The empowerment of private companies to the detriment of individuals obviously has profound consequences on democracy. As Crouch has pointed out, individuals have few positive rights to participate in the polity (2012, p. 13) – participating in the running of a local school, for example, as a member of the 'Big Society' is not the same as genuine political participation in the decision-making process. Of course it might be said that ordinary people were never really active participants in this process. Yet, their interests were to be represented by civil servants and elected representatives who at least in theory were motivated by the public interest. It is hard to believe that private companies are motivated by the same values. Even the civil service has changed dramatically under the New Public Management reforms introduced from the 1980s onwards to the extent that it has been 'colonised by business ideas, models and people so that its independence is moderated and its leaders are either constrained or replaced' (Wilks, 2013, p. 79). Furthermore, private companies have much more bargaining power than ordinary citizens, relying on the mobility of international capital to browbeat governments into submission. Yet, government is not just forced into capitulation by big business. They have come to share the same interests. As Wilks explains:

> The alliance with the political elite is of paramount importance. The corporate elite enjoys power, status and wealth; the political elite enjoys power, status and election. Both have high stakes in a system that generates income, wealth and the material benefits of economic growth. (2013, p. 115)

It is a symbiotic relationship in which one cannot survive without the other. Of course, both also need the masses onside as efficient workers, faithful voters and regular taxpayers. But, as this book has sought to demonstrate, they are co-opted rather than empowered. The result is a mere 'simulacrum of democracy' (Seymour, 2010, p. 16). Ordinary citizens do not even have the means necessary to hold the state accountable as the privatisation and contracting out process has meant that

DOI: 10.1057/9781137505781.0011

'government is responsible to the *demos* only for broad policy, not for detailed implementation' (Crouch, 2012, p. 102). For those who are subject to the most coercive measures of the State and find themselves stripped of the normal rights of citizenship – the 'precariat' (Standing, 2011) – there is a risk of the 'thinning of democracy' characterised by low voter turnout and the rising popularity of extremist right-wing parties which tap into popular fears and insecurities even more effectively than the mainstream parties (ibid., p. 147). This is evident in the United Kingdom with the recent electoral successes of UKIP.

In order to counter such trends and revive democracy, it is necessary to understand the political disaffection that leads some people to turn towards extremist right-wing parties. This entails not responding to authoritarian populist concerns about immigration, for example, but responding to sentiments of disempowerment and marginalisation from mainstream political processes. It is necessary to avoid pointing the finger of blame simply at whatever political party happens to be in power but at neoliberalism itself. Although this is a great challenge, it should not be insurmountable given that there is considerable disaffection with neoliberalism: it is just that few people tend to label it as such. Indeed, as Fisher and Gilbert have pointed out, writing in a recent publication for *Compass*, a left-wing think tank, the main problem with neoliberalism is the same as that which was thought to affect social democracy: the lack of empowerment of individual citizens (2014, p. 19). Both systems involved a significant degree of bureaucracy and often compulsion. Furthermore, neither was truly modern. As demonstrated earlier, neoliberalism has essentially been a restorationist project. It is necessary to exploit popular discontent and push open the cracks in the neoliberal hegemony. Yet, this must be done from below in order to avoid repeating the mistakes of the past.

There must be collective mobilisation for freedom. Yet, 'community' is not the starting point. As Standing explains, 'Freedom comes from being part of a community in which to realise freedom in the exercise of it. It is revealed through actions, not something granted from on high or divined in stone tablets' (2011, p. 167). Recognising this would hopefully enable a new democratic movement to avoid the pitfalls of 'community' as it was promoted via New Labour's communitarianism or the Coalition's 'Big Society'. In both cases, communities were often imagined as being tied together by common values, meaning that those who were deemed

DOI: 10.1057/9781137505781.0011

not to share those same values – the immigrant, the 'problem family', the welfare 'scrounger' – often found themselves excluded and citizens pitted against each other rather than able to work together. The idea of a genuinely new politics is 'not simply about empowering communities which already exist: it is also about enabling effective collectivities to come into existence' (Fisher & Gilbert, 2014, p. 10). While pluralism has been deliberately stifled by neoliberalism, the new politics could lead to a genuinely pluralist form of politics which would not just bring about citizen empowerment but also practical means of improving public policy by bringing 'more relevant information to bear on policies and also give those affected by policies a greater stake in making them work' (Bevir, 2010, p. 269). Such community activism already exists, as can be seen by the People's Assembly, a coalition of national and local campaign groups, protest movements and individual supporters. It organises demonstrations but also 'people's assemblies' whereby people can come together and make concrete policy proposals. Yet, these proposals have not so far been worked out in detail and they have not had any influence on government.

Popular mobilisation such as this needs to be tapped into and translated into practical politics. Think tanks such as *Compass* and the *New Economics Foundation* are seeking to influence the Labour Party to bring forward more radical, progressive, modern policies which would move politics beyond both the paternalistic State and the neoliberal State towards a truly democratic one. The discourse is not anti-statist: it is recognised that 'sympathetic governmental institutions' are needed to support such politics (Fisher & Gilbert, 2014, p. 19) and the State itself is of course needed to provide funding for public services and ensure equal access to those services. Yet, Labour has so far shown no signs of being able to offer a genuine democratic alternative, having signed up to the Conservative spending plans if re-elected and having failed to oppose many illiberal pieces of legislation during their time in opposition. If the Labour Party is to represent a genuine alternative, it would need to stop pandering to populism on issues such as immigration, and to demonstrate to the electorate that the real threat to their security and well-being lies elsewhere. It would also need to purge itself of neoliberalism. This is a formidable challenge, not just due to the continued hold of the ideology within the party, but also because it has now become a key feature of political common sense that it is impossible to win an election without

DOI: 10.1057/9781137505781.0011

the support of big business (Wilks, 2013, p. 71). Perhaps, in the short term at least, it is other left-wing political parties, such as the Greens or the new Left Unity Party, which offer the best prospect of change. While these parties are unlikely to make any significant headway in the 2015 General Election, they may at least exercise something of a 'UKIP-effect' on the Labour Party, forcing it to concede to some *popular* demands in the same way as the Conservative Party has been partly pushed by UKIP into implementing *populist* policies on immigration and Europe.

DOI: 10.1057/9781137505781.0011

Bibliography

Adam Smith International (2014) 'Devising a Strategy
    for State Enterprise Reform in Iraq', http://www.
    adamsmithinternational.com/case-study/state-enterprise-
    reform-in-iraq/, date accessed 27 October 2014.

Alexandre-Collier, Agnès (2010) *Les habits neufs de David
    Cameron: Les conservateurs britanniques 1990–2010* (Paris:
    Les Presses Sciences Po).

Alliance for Lobbying Transparency and Ethics
    Regulation (2009) *A Captive Commission: The role of the
    financial industry in shaping EU regulation*, http://www.
    alter-eu.org/sites/default/files/documents/a-captive-
    commission-5-11-09.pdf, date accessed 27 October
    2014.

Anderson, David (2014) *Terrorism Prevention and
    Investigation Measures in 2013: Second report of the
    independent reviewer on the operation of the Terrorism
    Prevention and Investigation Measures Act 2011* (London:
    HMSO).

Anderson, Paul & Mann, Nyta (1997), *Safety First: The
    making of new labour* (London: Granta Books).

Ashworth, Andrew & Zedner, Lucia (2014) *Preventive
    Justice* (Oxford: Oxford University Press).

Auda-André, Valérie (2014) 'The Coalition's Foreign
    Policy: A return to realism?' *Observatoire de la société
    britannique*, vol. 15, 245–254.

Aughey, Arthur (2005) 'Traditional Toryism', in Hickson,
    Kevin (ed.) *The Political Thought of the Conservative
    Party since 1945* (Basingstoke and New York: Palgrave
    Macmillan), pp. 7–27.

Ayers, Alison (2009) 'Imperial Liberties: Democratisation and governance in the "new" imperial order', *Political Studies*, vol. 57, 1–27.

Bale, Tim (2012) 'The Black Widow Effect: Why Britain's Conservative–Liberal Democrat coalition might have an unhappy ending', *Parliamentary Affairs*, vol. 65, 323–337.

Bale, Tim (2010) *The Conservative Party from Thatcher to Cameron* (Cambridge: Polity Press).

Bale, Tim & Hampshire, James (2012) 'Immigration Policy', in Heppell, Timothy & Seawright, David (eds) *Cameron and the Conservatives: The transition to coalition government* (Basingstoke and New York: Palgrave Macmillan), pp. 89–104.

Bale, Tim, Hampshire, James & Parto, Rebecca (2011) 'Having One's Cake and Eating It Too: Cameron's conservatives and immigration', *The Political Quarterly*, vol. 82 (3), 398–406.

Ball, James (2013) 'UK Jobs Soar – But How Many of These Jobs Are Real?' *The Guardian*, 15 January.

Barry, Norman (2005) 'New Right', in Hickson, Kevin (ed.) *The Political Thought of the Conservative Party since 1945* (Basingstoke and New York: Palgrave Macmillan), pp. 28–49.

Basu, Subhajit et al. (2014) 'An Open Letter from UK Internet Law Academic Experts to the UK Parliament', *The Guardian*, 15 July.

BBC (2014a) 'A Third of NHS Contracts Awarded to Private Firms – Report', *BBC News*, 10 December.

BBC (2014b) 'Clegg: UK can tackle terror threat within the law', *BBC News*, 2 September.

BBC (2012) 'G4S Loses Wolds Prison Contract', *BBC News*, 8 November.

Beech, Matt (2011a) 'A Tale of Two Liberalisms', in Lee, Simon & Beech, Matt (eds) *The Cameron-Clegg Government: Coalition politics in an age of austerity* (Basingstoke and New York: Palgrave Macmillan), pp. 267–279.

Beech, Matt (2011b) 'British Conservatism and Foreign Policy: Traditions and ideas shaping Cameron's global view', *British Journal of Politics and International Relations*, vol. 13, 348–363.

Beech, Matt & Munce, Peter (2014) 'The Place of Human Rights in Conservative Foreign Policy: Sceptics or enthusiasts?' Political Studies Association Annual Conference 2014, Midland Hotel, Manchester.

Bell, Emma (2011) *Criminal Justice and Neoliberalism* (Basingstoke and New York: Palgrave Macmillan).

DOI: 10.1057/9781137505781.0012

Bell, Emma (2013) 'The Prison Paradox in Neoliberal Britain', in Scott, David (ed.) *Why Prison?* (Cambridge: Cambridge University Press), pp. 44–64.

Bell, Emma (2014) 'The Antisociality of Antisocial Behaviour Policy', in Pickard, Sarah (ed.) *Anti-Social Behaviour in Britain: Victorian and contemporary perspectives* (Basingstoke and New York: Palgrave Macmillan), pp. 225–238.

Bell, Emma (*forthcoming*, 2016) 'From Marshallian Citizenship to Corporate Citizenship: The changing nature of citizenship in neoliberal Britain', *Revue française de la civilisation britannique*.

Bell, Stephen & Hindmoor, Andrew (2009) *Rethinking Governance: The centrality of the state in modern society* (Cambridge: Cambridge University Press).

Bennister, Mark & Heffernan, Richard (2014) 'The Limits to Prime Ministerial Autonomy: Cameron and the constraints of coalition', *Parliamentary Affairs*, vol. 67(1): 1–17.

Benyon, John (2011) 'The Con–Lib Agenda for Home Affairs', in Lee, Simon & Beech, Matt (eds) *The Cameron-Clegg Government: Coalition politics in an age of austerity* (Basingstoke and New York: Palgrave Macmillan), pp. 134–152.

Berman, Gavin (2012) *The August 2011 Riots: A statistical summary*, www.parliament.uk/briefing-papers/SN06099.pdf.

Berman, Gavin & Dar, Aliyah (2013) *Prison Population Statistics Standard Note: SN/SG/4334* (London: House of Commons Library).

Bevir, Mark (2010) *Democratic Governance* (Princeton and Oxford: Princeton University Press).

Binham, Caroline (2012) 'SFO Opted against Probe into Libor', *Financial Times*, June.

Blair, Tony (1997) 'Speech Made at the Aylesbury Estate', 2 June.

Blick, Andrew & Jones, George (2010) Written Evidence to the House of Lords Select Committee on the Constitution, The Cabinet Office and the Centre of Government, HL (2009–10) paper 30 (London: TSO, 2010).

Blunden, Tessa (2012) 'How We Are Using the Localism Act to Save Our Local Pub', *The Guardian,* 31 October.

Boffey, Daniel (2011) 'Academic Fury Over Order to Study the Big Society', *The Observer*, 27 March.

Bonefeld, Werner (2013) 'Human Economy and Social Policy: On ordo-liberalism and political authority', *History of Human Sciences,* vol. 26, 106–125.

DOI: 10.1057/9781137505781.0012

Bonefeld, Werner (2012) 'Freedom and the Strong State: German ordoliberalism', *New Political Economy*, 633–656.

Booth, Lorna (2014) *The 0.7% Aid Target*, House of Commons Library, Standard Note: SN/EP/3714 (London: HMSO).

Bowcott, Owen (2012) 'Government Considers Cutting Defendant Rights to Jury Trial', *The Guardian,* 16 January.

Bowling, Ben & Phillips, Coretta (2007) Disproportionate and Discriminatory: Reviewing the evidence on police stop and search, *The Modern Law Review*, vol. 70 (6), 936–961.

Brewer, Mike, Browne, James & Wenchao, Jin (2012) 'Universal Credit: A preliminary analysis of its impact on incomes and work incentives, *Fiscal Studies,* vol. 33 (1), 39–71.

British Influence (2014) *The British Influence Scorecard 2014: What influence does Britain have in the EU?* (London: British Influence).

Brockwell, Lord Butler of, (2010) *Hansard,* HL Debates, 6 July 2010, c. 145.

Bulpitt, Jim (1986) 'The Discipline of the New Democracy: Mrs Thatcher's domestic state-craft', *Political Studies*, vol. 34, 19–39.

Burchell, Graham, Gordon, Colin & Miller, Peter (1991) (eds) *The Foucault Effect: Studies in governmentality* (Chicago: University of Chicago).

Business, Innovation and Skills Committee (2014) *Royal Mail Privatisation* (London: HMSO).

Byrne, Ian & Weir, Stuart (2004) 'Democratic Audit: Executive democracy in war and peace', *Parliamentary Affairs* Vol. 57 n°2: 453–468.

Byrne, Christopher, Foster, Emma & Kerr, Peter (2012) 'Understanding Conservative Modernisation', in Heppell, Timothy & Seawright, David (eds) *Cameron and the Conservatives: The transition to coalition government* (Basingstoke and New York: Palgrave Macmillan), pp. 16–31.

Cameron, David (2014a) *Hansard,* HC Debates, 1 September, c. 26–27.

Cameron, David (2014b) 'Speech to the Conservative Party Conference', Birmingham, 1 October.

Cameron, David (2014c) *Hansard,* HC Debates, 26 September, c. 1264.

Cameron, David (2013a) 'Speech on Immigration', University Campus Suffolk, Ipswich, 25 March.

Cameron, David (2013b) 'Speech on the Economy', 7 March.

DOI: 10.1057/9781137505781.0012

Cameron, David (2013c) Speech cited in *The Telegraph,* 'David Cameron: Aid spending makes me proud to be British', 8 June.

Cameron, David (2013d) 'Speech on the Future of the EU and the UK's Relationship with It', *Bloomberg,* 23 January.

Cameron, David (2012a) 'Speech on Welfare Reform', Bluewater, Kent, 25 June.

Cameron, David (2012b) 'Speech on "Moral Capitalism"', New Zealand House, London, 19 January.

Cameron, David (2011a) 'Speech on the Big Society', 23 May.

Cameron, David (2011b) 'Speech on Welfare Reform Bill', London, 17 February.

Cameron, David (2011c) 'Speech on Multiculturalism', Munich, 5 February.

Cameron, David (2011d) 'Speech on the Fightback after the Riots', Witney, 15 August.

Cameron, David (2010a) 'Joint Press Conference with Nick Clegg', 10 Downing Street, 12 May.

Cameron, David (2010b) 'This Is a Radical Revolt against the Statist Approach of Big Government', *The Guardian,* 18 April.

Cameron, David (2010c) 'Speech on Education at the Centre Forum Think Tank', 8 December.

Cameron, David (2010d) 'Speech: Big Society vs Big Government', http://www.totalpolitics.com/print/speeches/35273/david-camerons-speaking-on-big-society-versus-big-government.thtml, date accessed 27 October 2014.

Cameron, David (2010e) 'Lobbying Speech', http://www.spinwatch.org/index.php/issues/lobbying/item/5579-the-next-big-scandal-cameron-s-lobbying-speech, date accessed 27 October 2014.

Cameron, David (2009) 'Big Society Can Fight Poverty. Big Government Just Fuels It', *The Guardian,* 10 November.

Cameron, David (2008) 'Leader's Speech to the Conservative Party Conference', Symphony Hall, Birmingham, 1 October.

Cameron, David (2006a) 'Balancing Freedom and Security – A Modern British Bill of Rights', speech to the Centre for Policy Studies, 26 June.

Cameron, David (2006b) 'Conservative Party Leader's Speech on Foreign Policy and National Security', speech to the British American Project, 11 September.

Cameron, David (2005) 'Leadership Victory Speech', London, 6 December.

DOI: 10.1057/9781137505781.0012

Cave, Tasmin (2013a) 'A Fake Register', 23 July, http://www.spinwatch.
org/index.php/issues/lobbying/item/5541-a-fake-register, date
accessed 27 October 2014.

Cave, Tasmin (2013b) 'More than a Lobby: Finance in the UK', *Open
Democracy,* 26 September.

Cave, Tasmin & Rowell, Andy (2014) *A Quiet Word: Lobbying, crony
capitalism and broken politics in Britain* (London: Random House).

CBI (Confederation of British Industry) (2013) *Our Global Future: The
business vision for a reformed EU* (London: CBI).

Centre for Social Justice (2009) *Dynamic Benefits: Towards welfare that
works* (London: Centre for Social Justice).

Chalmers, James (2014) '"Frenzied Law Making": Overcriminalization
by numbers', *Current Legal Problems,* vol. 67, 483–502.

Chalmers, Malcolm (2013) 'Mid-Term Blues? Defence and the 2013
Spending Review', Royal United Services Institute Briefing Paper,
https://www.rusi.org/, date accessed 27 October 2014.

Cheshire Constabulary (2014) 'How Can I Use CCTV to Keep my
Business Safe?' http://www.cheshire.police.uk/advice--information/
business-safety-security/cctv.aspx, date accessed 27 October 2014.

Civil Service (2014) *Indicators of Potential for Permanent Secretary
Roles,* http://news.bbc.co.uk/1/shared/bsp/hi/pdfs/07_07_14_
permanentsecretary.pdf, date accessed 27 October 2014.

Civil Service (2013) *Civil Service Reform Plan: One year on report*
(London: HMSO).

Civil Service (2010) *Civil Service Code* (London: HMSO).

Clarke, Becky (2014) 'I Would Give Up.... Chasing the "Reoffending
Rainbow"', *Criminal Justice Matters,* vol. 97.

Clarke, Greg (2011) 'Foreword', in Department for Communities and
Local Government, *A Plain English Guide to the Localism Act,* vol.1
(London: HMSO).

Clarke, John (2012) 'What Crisis Is This?' *Soundings,* 44–54.

Clarke, Kenneth (2010) 'The Government's Vision for Criminal Justice
Reform', speech to the centre for Crime and Justice Studies, 30 June.

Clegg, Nick (2014) 'PM and Deputy PM Speech on Emergency Security
Legislation', 10 Downing Street, 10 July.

Clegg, Nick (2011a) 'Speech to the Liberal Democrat Spring Conference',
Sheffield, 13 March.

Clegg, Nick (2011b) 'Speech on Restoring British Liberty', London,
7 January.

Clery, Elizabeth, Lee, Lucy & Kunz, Sarah (2013) *Public Attitudes to Poverty and Welfare: 1983–2011 analysis using British Social Attitudes* (London: Joseph Rowntree Foundation).

Coltart, Christopher (2014) 'Banking Act is a Paper Tiger', *Law Gazette*, 3 February.

Commission on a Bill of Rights (2012) *A UK Bill of Rights? The choice before us*, http://www.justice.gov.uk/about/cbr/index.htm, date accessed 27 October 2014.

Conservative Party (2014) *Protecting Human Rights in the UK: The Conservatives' proposals for changing Britain's human rights laws* (London: Conservative Party).

Conservative Party (2010) *Invitation to Join the Government of Britain* (London: Conservative Party).

Conservative Party (2009) *Reversing the Rise of the Surveillance State* (London: Conservative Party).

Constitution Unit (2011) *Inside Story: How coalition government works*, University College, London, http://www.ucl.ac.uk/constitution-unit/research/coalition-government/interim-report.pdf, date accessed 27 October 2014.

Corcoran, Mary & Hucklesby, Anthea (2013) *The Third Sector in Criminal Justice: Briefing Paper*, www.law.leeds.ac.uk/research/projects/the-third-sector-in-criminal-justice.php, date accessed 27 October 2014.

Corporate Europe Observatory (2014a) 'Regulating Finance: A necessary but "up-Hill" battle', 24 September, http://corporateeurope.org/financial-lobby/2014/09/regulating-finance-necessary-hill-battle, date accessed 27 October 2014.

Corporate Europe Observatory (2014b) *The Fire Power of the Financial Lobby: A survey of the size of the financial lobby at the EU level* (London: Corporate Europe Observatory).

Corporate Europe Observatory (2014c) 'TTIP: Debunking the Business Propaganda Over Investor Rights', 3 July, http://corporateeurope.org/international-trade/2014/07/ttip-debunking-business-propaganda-over-investor-rights, date accessed 27 October 2014.

Corporate Watch (2011) 'DFID Helps Bangladesh "Understand the Private Sector"', 15 July, http://www.corporatewatch.org.uk/?q=node/4020%3f, date accessed 27 October 2014.

Cowley, Philip & Stuart, Mark (2012) 'The Cambusters: The conservative European union referendum rebellion of October 2011', *The Political Quarterly*, vol. 83 (2), 402–406.

DOI: 10.1057/9781137505781.0012

Crouch, Colin (2012 [2004]) *Post-Democracy* (Cambridge: Policy Press).

Crouch, Colin (2010) 'The Global Firm: The problem of the giant firm in democratic capitalism', in Coen, David, Grant, Wyn & Wilson, Graham (eds) *The Oxford Handbook of Business and Government* (Oxford: Oxford University Press), pp. 148–172.

Crowe, Jessica (2011) 'The Government's Plans for Decentralisation and Localism: A progress report', *The Political Quarterly*, Vol. 82 (4) 651–657.

Czaikia, Mathias & De Haas, Hein (2013) *Determinants of Migration to the UK* (Oxford: Migration Observatory at the University of Oxford).

Daddow, Oliver (2013) 'The Use of Force in British Foreign Policy: From new labour to the coalition', *The Political Quarterly*, vol. 84 (1), 110–118.

Daddow, Oliver & Schnapper, Pauline (2013) 'Liberal Intervention in the Foreign Policy Thinking of Tony Blair and David Cameron', *Cambridge Review of International Affairs*, vol. 26 (2), 330–349.

Davie, Neil (2014) ' "La porte dérobée de l'eugénisme" entrouverte? Biologie, criminalité et justice pénale: bilan et tendances', in Prum, Michel (ed.) *Questions ethniques dans l'aire anglophone* (Paris: L'Harmattan), pp. 43–70.

Davoudi, Simin & Madanipour, Ali (2013) 'Localism and Neo-liberal Governmentality', *Town Planning Review*, vol. 84 (5), 551–562.

Dean, Mitchell (2010) (1999) *Governmentality: Power and rule in modern society* (London: Sage).

Department for Communities and Local Government (2012) *Creating the Conditions for Integration* (London: HMSO).

Department for Communities and Local Government (2011) *A Plain English Guide to the Localism Act* (London: HMSO).

Department for Education (2014) 'Open Academies and Academy Projects Awaiting Approval: November 2014', https://www.gov.uk/government/publications/open-academies-and-academy-projects-in-development, date accessed 10 December 2014.

Department for International development (2014) 'Helping Developing Countries' Economies to Grow', https://www.gov.uk/government/policies/helping-developing-countries-economies-to-grow/supporting-pages/helping-developing-countries-to-remove-barriers-to-trade-and-investment, date accessed 27 October 2014.

Department for International Development (2011) *The Engine of Development: The private sector and prosperity for poor people* (London: HMSO).

DOI: 10.1057/9781137505781.0012

Department of Health (2010) *Equity and Excellence: Liberating the NHS.* Cm 7881 (London: HMSO).

Dommett, Katharine (2013) 'A Miserable Little Compromise? Exploring Liberal Democrat Fortunes in the UK Coalition', *The Political Quarterly*, vol. 84 (2), 218–227.

Dorey, Peter (2011) *British Conservatism: The politics and philosophy of inequality* (London: I. B. Tauris).

Douzinas, Costas (2014) 'Human Rights and the Paradoxes of Liberalism', *Open Democracy*, 8 August, https://www.opendemocracy. net/costas-douzinas/human-rights-and-paradoxes-of-liberalism, date accessed 27 October 2014.

Downey, John, Stephens, Mike & Flaherty, Jan (2012) 'The "Sluice-gate" Public Sphere and the National DNA Database in the UK', *Media, Culture & Society*, vol. 34, 439–456.

Driver, Stephen (2011) 'Welfare Reform and Coalition Politics in the Age of Austerity', in Lee, Simon & Beech, Matt (eds) *The Cameron-Clegg Government: Coalition politics in an age of austerity* (Basingstoke and New York: Palgrave Macmillan), pp. 105–117.

Driver, Stephen (2009) ' "Fixing Our Broken Society": David Cameron's post-thatcherite social policy', in Lee, Simon & Beech, Matt (eds) *The Conservatives under David Cameron: Built to last?* (Basingstoke and New York: Palgrave Macmillan), pp. 80–96.

Duffy, Simon (2014) *Counting the Cuts: What the government doesn't want the public to know* (Sheffield: Centre for Welfare Reform).

Duncan Smith, Iain (2014) 'Speech on Welfare Reform', Centre for Social Justice, London, 23 January.

Dustmann, Christian & Frattini (2013) 'The Fiscal Effects of Immigration to the UK', Discussion Paper Series, Centre for Research and Analysis of Migration, CDP No 22/13 (London: University College).

Edwards, Jason (2012) 'Freedom, Free Institutions and the Big Society', *The Political Quarterly*, vol. 82 (1), 98–108.

Etzioni, Amitai (1995) *The Spirit of Community: Rights, responsibilities and the communitarian agenda* (London: Fontana Press).

European Committee of Social Rights (2014) *Conclusions, 2013: Great Britain*, Council of Europe, http://www.coe.int/t/dghl/monitoring/ socialcharter/conclusions/State/UKXX2_en.pdf, date accessed 27 October 2014.

Farnsworth, Kevin (2013) 'Public Policies for Private Corporations: The British corporate welfare state', *Renewal*, vol. 24 (4), 51–65.

DOI: 10.1057/9781137505781.0012

Farnsworth, Kevin (2006) 'Globalisation, Business and British Public Policy', *Contemporary Politics*, vol. 12 (1), 79–93.

Fisher, Mark & Gilbert, Jeremy (2014) *Reclaim Modernity: Beyond markets; beyond machines* (London: Compass).

Fisher, Rebecca (2013) 'The Insidious Nature of "Democracy Promotion"', in Fisher, Rebecca (ed.) *Managing Democracy, Managing Dissent: Capitalism, democracy and the organisation of consent* (London: Corporate Watch), pp. 334–356.

Flinders, Matthew (2006) 'Public/Private: The boundaries of the state', in Hay, Colin, Lister, Michael & Marsh, David, *The State: Theories and issues* (Basingstoke & New York: Palgrave Macmillan), pp. 223–247.

Foley, Michael (2000) *The British Presidency: Tony Blair and the politics of public leadership* (Manchester: Manchester University Press).

Foster, Emma Ann, Kerr, Peter & Byrne, Christopher (2014) 'Rolling Back to Roll Forward: Depoliticisation and the extension of government', *Policy & Politics*, vol. 42 (2), 225–241.

Foucault, Michel (1991) 'Governmentality', in Burchell, Graham, Gordon, Colin & Miller, Peter (eds) *The Foucault Effect: Studies in governmentality* (Chicago: University of Chicago Press), pp. 87–104.

Foucault, Michel (1975) *Surveiller et punir: naissance de la prison* (Paris: Gallimard).

Fox, Liam (2004) Cited in Pilbeam, Bruce (2005) 'Social Morality', in Hickson, Kevin (2005) (ed.) *The Political Thought of the Conservative Party since 1945* (Basingstoke and New York: Palgrave Macmillan), pp. 158–177.

Gamble, Andrew (2014) 'Austerity as Statecraft', *Parliamentary Affairs*, 1–16.

Gamble, Andrew (2012a) 'Economic Policy', in Heppell, Timothy & Seawright, David (eds) *Cameron and the Conservatives: The transition to coalition government* (Basingstoke and New York: Palgrave Macmillan), pp. 59–73.

Gamble, Andrew (2012b) 'Better Off Out? Britain and Europe', *The Political Quarterly*, vol. 83 (3), 68–77.

Gamble, Andrew (1994) *The Free Economy and the Strong State* (London: Macmillan).

Gay, Oonagh & Potton, Ed (2014) *FOI and Ministerial Vetoes,* House of Commons Library standard note SN/PC/05007 (London: HMSO).

Gilbert, Jeremy (2013a) 'What Kind of Thing is "Neoliberalism"?' *New Formations,* vol. 80/81, 7–22.

Gilbert, Jeremy (2013b) *Common Ground: Democracy and collectivity in an age of individualism* (London: Pluto Press).

Gove, Michael (2014) *Hansard*, HC Debates, 6 January, c. 3.

Grayling, Chris (2013) 'Speech to the Conservative Party Conference', 30 September.

Green, E. H. H. (2002) *Ideologies of Conservatism, Conservative Political Ideas in the Twentieth Century* (Oxford: Oxford University Press).

Greening, Justine (2014) 'Speech at Standard Chartered in London on the Focus of the UN's New Poverty Goals', 7 July.

Griffiths, Simon (2011) 'The Con–Lib Agenda in Education: Learning the hard way?', in Lee, Simon & Beech, Matt (eds) *The Cameron-Clegg Government: Coalition politics in an age of austerity* (Basingstoke and New York: Palgrave Macmillan), pp. 75–88.

Guardian Datablog (2013) '2013 Budget Briefing', http://www.theguardian.com/news/datablog/2010/apr/25/uk-public-spending-1963, date accessed 27 October 2014.

Guardian Datablog (2012) 'Why Is So Much UK Aid Money still Going to Companies Based in Britain?' http://www.theguardian.com/global-development/datablog/2012/sep/21/why-is-uk-aid-going-to-uk-companies, date accessed 27 October 2014.

Hague, William (2014) 'The Future of British Foreign Policy', speech to the Lord Mayor's Banquet, London, 15 April.

Hall, Stuart (2012) 'The Neoliberal Revolution', *Soundings*, vol. 48, 8–26.

Hall, Stuart (1988) *The Hard Road to Renewal: Thatcherism and the crisis of the left* (London and New York: Verso).

Hammond, Philip (2014) 'Speech to Conservative Party Conference 2014', 1 October.

Hamowy, Ronald (ed.) (2011) *The Constitution of Liberty: The definitive edition* (Chicago: University of Chicago Press).

Harcourt, Bernard (2011) *The Illusion of Markets: Punishment and the myth of natural order* (Cambridge and London: Harvard University Press).

Hardy, Henry (ed.) (2002) *Liberty: Isaiah Berlin* (Oxford: Oxford University Press).

Harvey, David (2007) *A Brief History of Neoliberalism*, 2nd edn (Oxford and New York: Oxford University Press).

Hay, Colin (2010) ' "Things Can Only Get Worse": The political and economic significance of 2010', *British Politics*, vol. 5 (4), 391–340.

Hayton, Richard (2014) 'Conservative Party Statecraft and the Politics of Coalition', *Parliamentary Affairs*, vol. 67, 6–24.

DOI: 10.1057/9781137505781.0012

Hayton, Richard (2010) 'Conservative Party Modernisation and David Cameron's Politics of the Family', *The Political Quarterly*, vol. 81 (4), 492–500.

Hayton, Richard (2013) 'Conservative Party Statecraft and the Politics of Coalition', *Parliamentary Affairs*, vol. 67, 6–24.

Hazell, Robert (2012) 'A Return to Cabinet Government', in Hazell, Robert and Yong, Ben, *Politics of Coalition: How the conservative-liberal democrat government works* (Oxford: Hart Publishing).

Head, Simon (2011) 'The Grim Threat to British Universities', *New York Review of Books*, 13 January.

Heffernan, Richard (2005) 'Why the Prime Minister Cannot be a President: Comparing institutional imperatives in Britain and America', *Parliamentary Affairs*, vol. 58 (1), 53–70.

Helm, Toby & Doward, Jamie (2014) 'Paddy Ashdown Slams "Kneejerk" Tory Response to Jihadi Terror Threat', *The Guardian*, 30 August.

Heppell, Timothy & Seawright, David (eds) (2012) *Cameron and the Conservatives: The transition to coalition government* (Basingstoke and New York: Palgrave Macmillan).

Hickman, Tom (2013) 'Turning out the Lights? The Justice and Security Act 2013', UK Const. L. Blog, 11 June, http://ukconstitutionallaw.org, date accessed 27 October 2014.

Hilary, John (2004) *Profiting from Poverty: Privatisation consultants, DFID and public services* (London: War on Want).

Hirsch, Donald & Hartfree, Yvette (2013) *Does Universal Credit Enable Households to Reach a Minimum Income Standard?* (London: Joseph Rowntree Foundation).

HM Government (2014) 'Creating Stronger and Safer Banks', https://www.gov.uk/government/policies/creating-stronger-and-safer-banks, date accessed 27 October 2014.

HM Government (2013) *A Guide to UK Taxation* (London: HMSO).

HM Government (2012) 'Huge Increase in Academies Takes Total to 2,300', https://www.gov.uk/government/news/huge-increase-in-academies-takes-total-to-more-than-2300, date accessed 10 December 2014.

HM Government (2011a) *Prevent Strategy*, Cm 8092 (London: HMSO).

HM Government (2011b) *Review of Counter-Terrorism and Security Powers*, Cm 8004 (London: HMSO).

HM Government (2010a) *The Coalition: Our programme for government* (London: HMSO).

DOI: 10.1057/9781137505781.0012

HM Government (2010b) *Breaking the Cycle: Effective punishment, rehabilitation and sentencing of offenders*, Cm 7972 (London: HMSO).

HM Treasury (2014) 'Public Expenditure Statistical Analyses 2014', cm 8902 (London: HMSO).

HMIC (Her Majesty's Inspectorate of Constabulary) (2013) *Stop and Search Powers: Are the police using them effectively and fairly?* (London: HMIC).

Hobhouse, L. T. (1911) *Liberalism* (Oxford: Oxford University Press).

Home Office (2013) *Surveillance Camera Code of Practice* (London: HMSO).

Home Office (2012) *Antisocial Behaviour Order Statistics: England and Wales, 2011* (London: HMSO).

Honeyman, Victoria (2012) 'Foreign Policy', in Heppell, Timothy & Seawright, David (eds) *Cameron and the Conservatives: The transition to coalition government* (Basingstoke and New York: Palgrave Macmillan), pp. 121–135.

Hopkins, Chris (2014) *Hansard*, HC Debates, 7 May, c. 185W.

Hopkins, Nick (2013) 'UK Gathering Secret Intelligence via Covert NSA Operation', *The Guardian*, 7 June.

House of Commons Committee of Public Accounts (2014) *Contracting Out Public Services to the Private Sector*, Forty-seventh Report of Session 2013–14 (London: HMSO).

House of Commons Public Administration Committee (2011) *The Big Society*, Seventeenth Report of Session 2010–12 (London: HMSO).

House of Lords (2014) *Persuasion and Power in the Modern World*, Report from the Select Committee on Soft Power and the UK's Influence (London: HMSO).

House of Lords Select Committee on the Constitution (2014) *Constitutional Implications of Coalition Government*, 5th Report of Session 2013–14 (London: HMSO).

Huhne, Chris (2009) 'A Bill to Save our Liberties', *The Guardian*, 26 February.

Hyde, John (2013) 'Osborne Imposes Further £142 Million of Cuts on MoJ', *The Law Society Gazette*, 18 March.

ICF GHK/Milieu (2013) *A Fact Finding Analysis on the Impact on the Member States' Social Security Systems of the Entitlements of Non-active Intra-EU Migrants to Special Non-contributory Cash Benefits and Healthcare Granted on the Basis of Residence*, http://ec.europa.eu/social/BlobServlet?docId=10972&langId=en, date accessed 27 October 2014.

DOI: 10.1057/9781137505781.0012

ICPS (2014) International Centre for Prison Studies, http://www.
prisonstudies.org/country/united-kingdom-england-wales, date
accessed 27 October 2014.

IMF (2010) International Monetary Fund 'World Economic Outlook
Database', https://www.imf.org/external/pubs/ft/weo/2010/01/
weodata/index.aspx, date accessed 27 October 2014.

IPSOS/MORI (2013) 'Attitudes to Healthcare Services in the UK',
29 November, http://www.ipsos-mori.com/researchpublications/
researcharchive/3305/Attitudes-to-healthcare-services-in-the-UK.
aspx, date accessed 27 October 2014.

Jenkin, Bernard (2014) 'Accountability and Leadership in Twenty-First
Century Whitehall', *The Political Quarterly,* vol. 85 (1) , 87–89.

Jenkins, Simon (2014) 'How Janus-faced George Osborne Defied
Stereotype and Triumphed', *The Guardian,* 16 April.

Joint Committee on Human Rights (2009) *Demonstrating Respect for
Rights? A human rights approach to policing protest,* Seventh Report of
Session 2008–09, HL Paper 47-I/HC 320-I (London: HMSO).

Joint Committee on Human Rights (2011) *Facilitating Peaceful Protest,*
Tenth Report (London: HMSO).

Joint Committee on Human Rights (2010) *Counter–Terrorism Policy
and Human Rights (Seventeenth Report): Bringing human rights back in,*
Sixteenth Report of Session 2009–10, HL Paper 86/HC 111 (London:
HMSO).

Jones, Chris (2014) *Back from the Battlefield: Domestic drones in the UK*
(London: Statewatch & Drone Wars UK).

Judicial Executive Board (2014) *Written Evidence on the Impact of the
Changes to Civil Legal Aid as Perceived by Judges* (London: Judicial
Executive Board).

Justice Measures (2012) 'Custodial Sentence Length', http://www.
justicemeasures.co.uk/trend/Custodial_sentence_length_(months).
aspx?pt=a&a=0&dt=undefined, date accessed 27 October 2014.

Keeling, Ruth (2013) 'Power of Competence Restrictions Criticised',
Local Government Chronicle, 23 July.

Kerr, Peter, Byrne, Christopher & Foster, Emma (2011) 'Theorising
Cameron', *Political Studies Review,* vol. 9, 193–207.

King, A. (1975) 'Overload: Problems of governing in the 1970s', *Political
Studies,* vol. 23 (2 & 3), 162–174.

King, Peter (2011) *The New Politics: Liberal conservatism or same old Tories?*
(Bristol: The Policy Press).

DOI: 10.1057/9781137505781.0012

King, Roger (2007) *The Regulatory State in an Age of Governance: Soft words and big sticks* (Basingstoke & New York: Palgrave Macmillan).

Kober-Smith, Anémone (2014) 'Le government de coalition et le secteur de la santé : une politique contestée', *Observatoire de la société britannique*, vol. 15, 115–128.

Kundnani, Arun (2012) 'Multiculturalism and its Discontents: Left, right and liberal', *European Journal of Cultural Studies*, vol. 15 (2), 155–166.

Kundnani, Arun (2009) *Spooked: How not to prevent violent extremism* (London: Institute of Race Relations).

Laws, David (2012) 'The Orange Book: Eight years on', *Economic Affairs*, 31–35.

Lee, Simon (2011) ' "We Are All in This Together": The coalition agenda for British modernization', in Lee, Simon & Beech, Matt (eds) *The Cameron-Clegg Government: Coalition politics in an age of austerity* (Basingstoke and New York: Palgrave Macmillan), pp. 3–23.

Lee, Simon & Beech, Matt (eds) (2011) *The Cameron-Clegg Government: Coalition politics in an age of austerity* (Basingstoke and New York: Palgrave Macmillan).

Lee, Simon & Beech, Matt (eds) (2009) *The Conservatives under David Cameron: Built to last?* (Basingstoke and New York: Palgrave Macmillan).

Leeder, Adam & Mabbett, Deborah (2012) 'Free Schools: Big Society or Small Interests?' *The Political Quarterly*, vol. 82 (1), 133–144.

Letwin, Oliver (2002a) 'The Moral Market: Why conservatives believe in social capital', speech delivered to the Centre for Policy Studies at the Conservative Party Conference, 8 October.

Letwin, Oliver (2002b) *The Frontline Against Fear: Taking neighbourhood policing seriously* (London: The Bow Group).

Lewis, Leigh (2014) 'Civil Service Reform: Trust on trial', *The Political Quarterly*, vol. 85 (1), 84–86.

Liberal Democrats (2014) 'Protecting Civil Liberties', http://www.libdems. org.uk/protecting_civil_liberties, date accessed 27 October 2014.

Liberal Democrats (2010) *Manifesto* (London: Liberal Democrats).

Liberty (2011) 'Liberty's Second Reading Briefing on the Protection of Freedoms Bill in the House of Commons', https://www.liberty-human-rights.org.uk, date accessed 27 October 2014.

Lister, Michael & Marsh, David (2006) 'Conclusion', in Hay, Colin, Lister, Michael & Marsh, David, *The State: Theories and issues* (Basingstoke and New York: Palgrave Macmillan), pp. 248–261.

DOI: 10.1057/9781137505781.0012

London Councils (2013) *Tracking Welfare Reform: The impact of housing benefit (LHA) reform in London* (London: London Councils).

Lord Hailsham (1976) 'The Richard Dimbleby Lecture', *BBC*, 14 October.

Lord McFall of Alcluith (2013) *Hansard*, House of Lords Debates, 24 July, Col. 1359–1362.

Lord Thomas of Cwmgiedd (2014) 'Reshaping Justice', speech to the organisation 'JUSTICE', 3 March.

Low Pay Commission (2014) *National Minimum Wage: Low pay commission report 2014*, Cm 8816 (London: HMSO).

Lynch, Philip (2012) 'European Policy', in Heppell, Timothy & Seawright, David (eds) *Cameron and the Conservatives: The transition to coalition government* (Basingstoke and New York: Palgrave Macmillan), pp. 74–88.

Lynch, Philip (2011) 'The Con–Lib Agenda for Europe', in Lee, Simon & Beech, Matt (eds) *The Cameron-Clegg Government: Coalition politics in an age of austerity* (Basingstoke and New York: Palgrave Macmillan), pp. 218–236.

Lynch, Philip (2009) 'The Conservatives and the European Union: The lull before the storm?' in Lee, Simon and Beech, Matt (eds) *The Conservatives under David Cameron*, (Basingstoke and New York: Palgrave Macmillan), pp. 187–207.

Mabbett, Deborah (2013) 'The Second Time as Tragedy? Welfare Reform under Thatcher and the Coalition', *The Political Quarterly*, vol. 84 (1), 43–52.

Macartney, Huw (2011) 'Crisis for the State or Crisis of the State?' *The Political Quarterly*, vol. 82 (2), 193–203.

MacDonald, Lord (2011) *Review of Counter-Terrorism and Security Powers*, Cm 8003 (London: HMSO).

MacInnes, Tom, Aldridge, Hannah, Bushe, Sabrina, Kenway, Peter & Tinson, Adam (2013) *Monitoring Poverty and Social Exclusion 2013* (London: Joseph Rowntree Foundation).

Malik, Shiv (2013) 'Activists Are Intimidating Charities into Quitting Work Scheme, Says DWP', *The Guardian*, 27 February 2013.

Marquand, David (1988) *The Unprincipled Society: New demands and old politics* (London: Jonathan Cape).

Marsh, David (2002) 'Pluralism and the Study of British Politics: It is always the happy hour for men with money, knowledge and power', in Hay, Colin (ed.), British Politics Today (Cambridge: Polity Press).

DOI: 10.1057/9781137505781.0012

Marshall, Paul & Laws, David (2004) *The Orange Book: Reclaiming liberalism* (London: Profile Books).

Mathiason, Nick & Bessaoud, Yuba (2011) 'Tory Party Funding from City Doubles under Cameron', *Bureau of Investigative Journalism*, 8 February.

Mathiesen, Thomas (2013) *Towards a Surveillant Society: The rise of surveillance systems in Europe* (Hook: Waterside Press).

Mathiesen, Thomas (1997) 'The Viewer Society: Michel Foucault's "Panopticon" Revisited', *Theoretical Criminology*, vol. 1, 215–234.

Maude, Francis (2011) Evidence provided to the House of Commons Public Administration Select Committee, *The Big Society: Seventeenth report of session 2010–12*, vol. 1, 12 October.

May, Theresa (2014a) *Hansard*, HC Debates, 30 April, c. 831.

May, Theresa (2014b) 'Speech to the Conservative Party Conference', 30 September.

May, Theresa (2010a) *Hansard*, HC Deb, 13 July, c.797.

May, Theresa (2010b) 'Moving Beyond the ASBO', speech delivered at the Coin Street Community Centre, London, 28 July.

McAnulla, Stuart (2012) 'Liberal Conservatism: Ideological coherence?', in Heppell, Timothy & Seawright, David (eds) *Cameron and the Conservatives: The transition to coalition government* (Basingstoke and New York: Palgrave Macmillan), pp. 166–180.

Merrick, Jane (2013) 'Secret Memo Shows Michael Gove's Plan for Privatisation of Academies', *The Independent*, 10 February.

Miliband, Ed (2010) Speech delivered 15 May.

Mill, John Stuart (1869) *On Liberty* (London: Longman, Roberts & Green).

Miller, David & Dinan, William (2009) *Revolving Doors, Accountability and Transparency – Emerging Regulatory Concerns and Policy Solutions in the Financial Crisis*, a report commissioned by the OECD, May.

Ministry of Justice (2014a) *New Criminal Offences England and Wales 1st June 2009 – 31st May 2013: Statistics bulletin* (London: HMSO).

Ministry of Justice (2014b) 'Population Bulletin: Weekly, 26 September', https://www.gov.uk/government/uploads/system/uploads/attachment_data/file/358718/prison-population-figures-26-sept-2014.xls, date accessed 27 October 2014.

Ministry of Justice (2013) *Transforming Rehabilitation: A revolution in the way we manage offenders* (London: HMSO).

Montgomerie, Tim (2012) 'Ten Things You Need to Know about the Group of Four that Runs the Coalition', *Conservative Home*, 16 February 2012, http://www.conservativehome.com/thetorydiary/2012/02/

DOI: 10.1057/9781137505781.0012

ten-things-you-need-to-know-about-the-group-of-four-that-runs-the-coalition.html, date accessed 27 October 2014.

Moore, John & Scott, David (2012) 'It's Not Just about Profits: Privatisation, social enterprise and the "John Lewis" prison', *Criminal Justice Matters*, vol. 87 (1), 42–43.

Moran, M. (2007) *The British Regulatory State: High modernism and hyper-innovation* (Oxford and New York: Oxford University Press).

Mount, Ferdinand (2013 [2012]) *The New Few or a Very British Oligarchy* (London: Simon & Schuster).

Munce, Peter (2012) 'Profoundly Un-Conservative? David Cameron and the UK Bill of Rights Debate', *The Political Quarterly*, vol. 83 (1), 60–68.

NAO (National Audit Office) (2014) *The Work Programme* (London: National Audit Office).

NAO (National Audit Office) (2013a) *The Role of Major Contractors in the Delivery of Public Services*, HC 810 (London: National Audit Office).

NAO (National Audit Office) (2013b) *The Ministry of Justice's Electronic Monitoring Contracts*, HC 737 (London: National Audit Office).

NAO (National Audit Office) (2010) *Maintaining the Financial Stability of UK Banks: Update on the support schemes,* report by the Comptroller and Auditor General (London: National Audit Office).

NatCen (2013) *British Social Attitudes 2013: Attitudes to immigration* (London: NatCen).

Neocleous, Mark (2007) 'Security, Liberty and the Myth of Balance: Towards a critique of security politics', *Contemporary Political Theory*, vol. 6, 131–149.

New Policy Institute (2013) *London's Poverty Profile*, http://www.londonspovertyprofile.org.uk/LPP_2013_Report_Web.pdf, date accessed 27 October 2014.

Norman, Jesse (2010) *The Big Society* (Buckingham: University of Buckingham Press).

Norman, Jesse & Ganesh, Janan (2006) *Compassionate Conservatism: What it is, why we need it* (London: Policy Exchange).

Nye, Joseph (2004) *Soft Power: The means to success in world politics* (New York: Public Affairs).

OECD (2014) Organisation for Economic Cooperation and Development, 'Economic Forecast Summary', http://www.oecd.org/eco/outlook/united-kingdom-economic-forecast-summary.htm, date accessed 27 October 2014.

DOI: 10.1057/9781137505781.0012

One3One Solutions (2014) http://one3one.justice.gov.uk/, date accessed 27 October 2014.

ONS (Office for National Statistics) (2014a) *Labour Market Statistics, June 2014* (London: ONS).

ONS (Office for National Statistics) (2014b) *Migration Statistics Quarterly Report, May 2014* (London: ONS).

Osborne, George (2012) 'Speech to the Conservative Party Conference', Birmingham, 8 October.

Osborne, George (2010a) Cited in Baker, Alex & Parker, George, 'Osborne Talks Tough on Cutting Benefits', *Financial Times*, 9 September.

Osborne, George (2010b) 'Speech to the House of Commons Introducing the Emergency Budget', 22 June.

Osborne, David & Gaebler, Ted (1993) *Reinventing Government: How the entrepreneurial spirit is transforming the public sector* (New York: Plume).

Osborne, Peter (2008 [2007]) *The Triumph of the Political Class* (London: Simon & Schuster).

Page, Robert M. (2011) 'The Emerging Blue (and Orange) Health Strategy: Continuity or change?', in Lee, Simon & Beech, Matt (eds) *The Cameron-Clegg Government: Coalition politics in an age of austerity* (Basingstoke and New York: Palgrave Macmillan), pp. 89–104.

Park, Alison, Clery, Elizabeth, Curtice, John, Phillips, Miranda & Utting, David (2012) *British Social Attitudes 29* (London: NatCen Social Research).

Parker, George (2014) 'David Cameron Does Not Rule out Cutting Top Rate of Income Tax', *Financial Times*, 29 January.

Parker, George & Warrell, Helen (2014) 'Gove Takes Aim at Cameron's Etonians', *Financial Times*, 14 March.

Parliamentary Commission on Banking Standards (2013) *Changing Banking for Good: First report of session 2013-14*, vol. II, HL Paper 27-II HC 175-II (London: HMSO).

Patel, Ramesh (2012) 'Finally Exposed! The Deficit Myth', *The Huffington Post*, 24 October.

Peters, Guy (1997) 'Shouldn't Row, Can't Steer: What's a government to do?' *Public Policy and Administration*, vol. 12, 51–61.

Peters, Guy & Pierre, Jon (2006) 'Governance, Government and the State', in Hay, Colin, Lister, Michael & Marsh, David, *The State: Theories and issues* (Basingstoke and New York: Palgrave Macmillan), pp. 209–222.

DOI: 10.1057/9781137505781.0012

Pickard, Sarah (2014) 'Keep Them Kettled! Student Protests, Policing and Anti-social Behaviour', in Pickard, Sarah (ed.) *Anti-Social Behaviour in Britain: Victorian and contemporary perspectives* (Basingstoke and New York: Palgrave Macmillan), pp. 77–91.

Pipe, Jules (2013) 'Two Years on, What Has the Localism Act Achieved?' *The Guardian*, 2 November.

Porter, Henry (2008) 'Why I told Parliament: You've failed us on liberty', *The Observer*, Sunday 9 March.

Pratt, John, Brown, David, Brown, Mark, Hallsworth, Simon & Morrison, Wayne (eds) (2005) *The New Punitiveness: Trends, theories, perspectives* (Cullompton: Willan Publishing).

Prieg, Lydia & Greenham, Tony (2011) *Feather-bedding Financial Services: Are British banks getting hidden subsidies?* (London: New Economics Foundation).

Raab, Dominic (2009) *The Assault on Liberty: What went wrong with rights* (London: Fourth Estate).

Rees, James, Whitworth, Adam & Carter, Eleanor (2013) 'Support for all in the UK Work Programme? Differential payments, same old problem...', *Third Sector Research Centre Working Paper 115*, http://www.birmingham.ac.uk/generic/tsrc/documents/tsrc/working-papers/working-paper-115.pdf, date accessed 27 October 2014.

Reeve, John (2013) 'BSIA Attempts to Clarify Question of How Many CCTV Cameras There Are in the UK', http://www.securitynewsdesk.com/2013/07/11/bsia-attempts-to-clarify-question-of-how-many-cctv-cameras-in-the-uk/, date accessed 27 October 2014.

Reiner, R. (2007) *Law and Order: An honest citizen's guide to crime and control* (Cambridge and Malden: Polity Press).

Rhodes, R. A. W. (1996) 'The New Governance: Governing without government', *Political Studies*, vol. 44, 652–667.

Rhodes, R. A. W. (1994) 'The Hollowing Out of the State: The changing nature of the public service in Britain', *Political Quarterly*, 138–151.

Richardson, Diane (2005) 'Desiring Sameness? The Rise of a Neoliberal Politics of Normalisation', Antipode, vol. 37 (3), pp. 515–535.

Rigby, Elizabeth (2014) 'Lib Dems Plan Freedom of Information Rules for Private Companies', *Financial Times*, 15 August.

Robb, George (2002) *White-collar Crime in Modern England: Financial fraud and business morality 1845–1929* (Cambridge: Cambridge University Press).

DOI: 10.1057/9781137505781.0012

Robin, Corey (2011) *The Reactionary Mind: Conservatism from Edmund Burke to Sarah Palin* (Oxford: Oxford University Press).

Rose, Nikolas (1999) *Powers of Freedom: Reframing political thought* (Cambridge: Cambridge University Press).

Rose, Nikolas (1996) 'Governing "Advanced" Liberal Democracies', in Barry, Andrew, Osborne, Thomas & Rose, Nikolas (eds) *Foucault and Political Reason: Liberalism, neo-liberalism and rationalities of government* (Chicago: University of Chicago), pp. 37–64.

Rustin, Michael and Massey, Doreen (2014) 'Rethinking the Neoliberal World Order' in Hall, Stuart, Massey, Doreen and Rustin, Michael (eds) *After Neoliberalism: The Kilburn Manifesto* (London: Lawrence and Wishart).

Sampson, Antony (2005) *Who Runs this Place? An anatomy of Britain in the 21st Century* (London: John Murray).

Sandford, Mark (2013) 'Localism Act: Assets of community value' (London: House of Commons Library).

Scheuerman, William E. (1999) *Carl Schmitt: The end of law twentieth century political thinkers* (Lanham & Oxford: Rowman & Littlefield).

Scott, Peter & Williams, Steve (2014) 'The Coalition Government and Employment Relations: Accelerated neoliberalism and the rise of employer-dominated voluntarism', *Observatoire de la Société Britannique*, vol. 15, 145–164.

Seldon, Anthony (2011) 'Inside Cameron's Number 10', *Parliamentary Brief*, April.

Senellart, Michel (ed.) (2008 [2004]) *Michel Foucault: The birth of biopolitics* (Basingstoke & New York: Palgrave Macmillan).

Seymour, Richard (2010) *The Meaning of David Cameron* (Winchester & Washington DC: Zero Books).

Shildrick, Tracy, MacDonald, Robert, Furlong, Andy, Roden, Johann & Crow, Robert (2012) *Are 'Cultures of Worklessness' Passed Down the Generations?* (London: Joseph Rowntree Foundation).

Shutt, Harry (2012) 'Keynes Is the Problem, Not the Solution', *The Economist*, 21 August.

Sikka, Prem (2011) 'HMRC Has a Cosy Relationship with the Tax Avoidance Industry', *The Guardian,* 20 December.

Skelcher, Chris (2000) 'Changing images of the State: Overloaded, hollowed-out, congested', *Public Policy and Administration*, vol. 15 (3), 3–19.

DOI: 10.1057/9781137505781.0012

Skinner, Quentin (2014) 'Liberty, Liberalism and Surveillance: An interview with Quentin Skinner' by Richard Marshall in White, Stuart & Seth-Smith Niki 'Democratic Wealth: Building a Citizens' Economy', *Open Democracy*, https://www.smashwords.com/books/view/416267, date accessed 27 October 2014.

Slay, Julia & Penny, Joe (2013) *Surviving Austerity: Local voices and local action in England's poorest neighbourhoods* (London: New Economics Foundation).

Smith, Louise (2014) *Neighbourhood Planning* (London: House of Commons Library).

Smith, Martin (2006) 'Pluralism', in Hay, Colin, Lister, Michael & Marsh, David (eds), *The State: Theories and issues* (Basingstoke and New York: Palgrave Macmillan), pp. 21–38.

Sowells, Nicholas (2014) 'The Coalition's Economic Policy of Fiscal Austerity and Monetary Experimentation by the Bank of England', *Observatoire de la société britannique*, vol. 15, 165–188.

Standing, Guy (2011) *The Precariat: The new dangerous class* (London: Bloomsbury Academic).

Survation/Progressive Polling (2013) *Political Issues Survey*, 6 May, http://survation.com/wp-content/uploads/2014/05/Progressive-Polling-Political-Issues-Survey.pdf, date accessed 27 October 2014.

Synetics (2014) *CCTV Perceptions and Beliefs: UK public space research 2014*, http://www.synecticsuk.com/research, date accessed 27 October 2014.

Tansey, Rachel (2012) 'Brits Are Best at Lobbying the EU...to What End?' *Open Democracy*, 13 December 2012.

Tatchell, Peter (2013) 'Why Our New Same-sex Marriage Is Not yet Equal marriage', *The New Statesman*, 19 July.

Teague, Michael (2013) 'Rehabilitation, Punishment and Profit: The dismantling of public-sector probation', *British Society of Criminology Newsletter*, No. 72, 15–19.

Thaler, Richard & Sunstein, Cass (2008) *Nudge: Improving decisions about health, wealth, and happiness* (London: Penguin).

Thatcher, Margaret (2001) 'Tony Blair is Committed to the Extinction of Britain', *The Telegraph*, 1 June.

Thatcher, Margaret (1992) 'The Principles of Thatcherism', speech in Seoul, South Korea, 3 September.

The Financial Times (2012) 'Wheatley's Libor Detoxification', 30 September.

The Telegraph (2014) 'UK Economy: Voters put trust in Tories', 1 February.

The Telegraph (2012) 'We Need Drone Aircraft, Says Police Chief', 1 October.

Thomas, Paul (2013) 'Preventing Violent Extremism under the Coalition', *Public Spirit*, 16 December, http://www.publicspirit.org.uk/

Thomas, Paul (2010) 'Failed and Friendless: The UK's "preventing violent extremism"', *The British Journal of Politics and International Relations*, vol. 12, 442–458.

Timms, Stephen (2014) *Hansard,* HC Debates, 3 April, c. 1076.

Toynbee, Polly & Walker, David (2012) *Dogma & Disarray: Cameron at half-time* (London: Granta).

Travis, Alan (2014) 'UN Commissioner Criticises Decision to Fast-track Emergency Surveillance Bill', *The Guardian,* 16 July.

TUC (2011) Evidence submitted to the Public Administration Committee, *The Big Society: Seventeenth report of session 2010–12* (London: HMSO).

Vargas-Silva, Carlos (2014)' Long-Term International Migration Flows to and from the UK', *Migration Observatory*, 20 February, http://www.migrationobservatory.ox.ac.uk/briefings/long-term-international-migration-flows-and-uk.

Vickers, Rhiannon (2011) 'The Con–Lib Agenda for Foreign Policy and International Development', in Lee, Simon & Beech, Matt (eds) *The Cameron-Clegg Government: Coalition politics in an age of austerity* (Basingstoke and New York: Palgrave Macmillan), pp. 203–217.

Walker, David (2012) 'Response to Roy Hattersley and Kevin Hickson', *Political Quarterly*, vol. 83 (1), 16–17.

Watt, Nicholas (2014) 'David Cameron Welcomes German Proposals on EU Migration Rules', *The Guardian*, 27 March.

Watt, Nicholas (2009) 'David Cameron Apologises to Gay People for Section 28', *The Guardian,* 2 July.

Weir, Stuart & Beetham, David (1999) *Political Power and Democratic Control in Britain: The democratic audit of the United Kingdom* (London and New York: Routledge).

Westminster Foundation for Democracy (2014) 'The Westminster Consortium for Parliaments and Democracy', http://www.wfd.org, date accessed 27 October 2014.

Whal, Peter (2014) 'A Paper Tiger: The new EU draft regulations on banking structure', *EU Financial Reforms Newsletter,* issue 22, February, date accessed 27 October 2014.

DOI: 10.1057/9781137505781.0012

Whyte, David (2007) 'The Crimes of Neoliberal Rule in Occupied Iraq', *British Journal of* Criminology, vol. 47, 177–195.

Wilks, Stephen (2013) *The Political Power of the Business Corporation* (Cheltenham: Edward Elgar).

Willetts, David (2005) 'Speech on Compassionate Conservatism and the War on Poverty', January 6.

Willetts, David (1994) *Civic Conservatism* (London: Social Market Foundation).

Williams, Stephen (2014) *Hansard*, HC Debates, 17 July, c. 805W.

Wintour, Patrick (2013) 'How David Cameron's Approach to Foreign Intervention is Evolving', *The Guardian,* 1 February.

YouGov (2013) 'Two Thirds of Public Oppose Royal Mail Sell-Off', http://yougov.co.uk/news/2013/07/11/two-thirds-public-oppose-royal-mail-sell/, date accessed 27 October 2014.

YouGov (2012) 'Are Changes to Welfare Benefits, Pensions and Taxes Needed?' http://www.prospectmagazine.co.uk, date accessed 27 October 2014.

Young, Jock (1999) *The Exclusive Society* (London: Sage).

DOI: 10.1057/9781137505781.0012

Index

NDNAD (National DNA Database), 46
New Labour, *see* Labour Party
new liberalism, 26, 100

Orange Book, 27, 102, 103
ordoliberalism, 35, 107, 108, 109
Osborne, George, 9, 10, 27, 34,
    68, 69, 70

paternalism, 19
planning, 22, 23, 105
pluralism, 13
Policy Exchange, 26
prevent strategy, 39, 40
privatisation, 23, 63, 65, 66, 69, 72, 81,
    83, 88, 89, 102
protest, right to, 56

regulation of financial services, 75, 76
Royal Mail, 73, 81, 102

secret courts, 60
social liberalism, 26, 41–2, 96, 100
Spending Review, 20
statecraft, 96, 102–6
surveillance, 39, 44, 46–51, 56, 57, 64,
    66, 105

Thatcher, Margaret, 8, 16, 26, 27, 36,
    45, 72, 82, 89, 97, 99, 103, 106,
    107, 109

Universal Credit, 28, 29, 30, 32

work programme, 28–31, 72

DOI: 10.1057/9781137505781.0013